Learn JavaScript with p5.js

Coding for Visual Learners

Engin Arslan

Apress®

Learn JavaScript with p5.js: Coding for Visual Learners

Engin Arslan
Toronto, Ontario, Canada

ISBN-13 (pbk): 978-1-4842-3425-9   ISBN-13 (electronic): 978-1-4842-3426-6
https://doi.org/10.1007/978-1-4842-3426-6

Library of Congress Control Number: 2018935139

Managing Director, Apress Media LLC: Welmoed Spahr
Acquisitions Editor: Natalie Pao
Development Editor: James Markham
Coordinating Editor: Jessica Vakili

Cover designed by eStudioCalamar

Cover image designed by Freepik (www.freepik.com)

Distributed to the book trade worldwide by Springer Science+Business Media New York, 233 Spring Street, 6th Floor, New York, NY 10013. Phone 1-800-SPRINGER, fax (201) 348-4505, e-mail orders-ny@springer-sbm.com, or visit www.springeronline.com. Apress Media, LLC is a California LLC and the sole member (owner) is Springer Science + Business Media Finance Inc (SSBM Finance Inc). SSBM Finance Inc is a **Delaware** corporation.

For information on translations, please e-mail rights@apress.com, or visit http://www.apress.com/rights-permissions.

Apress titles may be purchased in bulk for academic, corporate, or promotional use. eBook versions and licenses are also available for most titles. For more information, reference our Print and eBook Bulk Sales web page at http://www.apress.com/bulk-sales.

Any source code or other supplementary material referenced by the author in this book is available to readers on GitHub via the book's product page, located at www.apress.com/978-1-4842-3425-9. For more detailed information, please visit http://www.apress.com/source-code.

Printed on acid-free paper

Table of Contents

About the Author

Engin Arslan is a Software Developer with a Bachelor of Science in
Materials Engineering and a Postgraduate Degree in Visual Effects. Before
becoming a Developer, he worked as a Visual Effects Artist / Technical
Director on films and TV shows including *Resident Evil, Tron, Mama,
Pompeii, Vikings,* and *Strai*n. He received an Emmy nomination and won a
Canadian Screen Award for his achievements in Visual Effects. During his
time in VFX, he fell in love with Python and with programming in general.
As a result, he changed careers to be able to immerse himself completely
in software development. Engin currently works at a Toronto-based digital
services company, where he helps develop solutions in strategic problem
spaces using emerging technologies. He also works at Seneca College as
a part-time professor and creates online courses for Lynda/LinkedIn and
Pluralsight.

About This Book

The emphasis of this book will be primarily on learning programming using JavaScript and p5.js and secondarily in creating visuals. The main focus is to teach you how to program so that you can choose to pursue whatever field that you would like with your newly established skill set. The skills that you will acquire from this book are highly transferrable and can be used with whatever you choose to build: whether web applications, programmable robots, or generative art. This means that I will provide you with enough context so that you can build a strong foundation for programming. But I also won't hinder your momentum with irrelevant technical or theoretical points. The aim is to build a strong but a minimum viable knowledge to get you running with coding. This is the book that I wished I had available when I was learning coding myself.

If you are an artist or a visual designer, this book is perfect for you as you might find the examples we will be building to be directly relevant to your work. If not, this is still a great book for learning programming as the visual nature of the exercises will help you grasp the fundamentals of programming more easily and let you build a strong foundation in a shorter amount of time.

This book will present various JavaScript and p5.js features and concepts in the following chapters. The knowledge will be reinforced by building several useful examples like an animation and a data visualization; and as a final project, we will be building a game that can be deployed online using what we learned in this book!

Here is a rundown of the topics that we will be covering:

Chapter 1 - Introduction: Provides an overview of coding versus programming.

Chapter 2 - Getting Started: We will learn some very basic JavaScript commands and operations to get started with using p5.js.

Chapter 3 - Colors in p5.js: This will be a p5.js-specific chapter where we learn about how colors are defined and used in p5.js. This doesn't pertain to JavaScript but needs to be explored regardless to be able to use p5.js in a comfortable manner.

Chapter 4 - Operations and Variables: We will make use of the JavaScript knowledge we acquired in the second chapter in p5.js context.

Chapter 5 - Conditional Statements and Comparison Operators: This chapter will allow us to write programs that can respond to different conditions by using conditionals and comparison operators.

Chapter 6 - More p5.js Variables: This will be another p5.js-specific chapter where we will learn about several library-specific variables.

Chapter 7 - Loops: Here we will learn about loops, which will allow us to build programs that handle enormous amounts of calculations.

Chapter 8 - Functions: Functions are the building blocks of JavaScript and we will learn more about them in order to build more scalable, modular, and robust programs.

Chapter 9 - Objects and **Chapter 10 - Arrays**: Objects and Arrays are JavaScript data structures that will allow us to organize our code and handle complexity in more intelligent ways.

Chapter 11 - Events: Event handling will allow us to write programs that handles user interaction.

Chapter 12 - More on p5.js: Another p5.js-only chapter where we learn more about library-specific features before diving into our final project.

Chapter 13 - Final Project: We will build a game using everything we have learned up to this chapter!

CHAPTER 1

Introduction

At this age and time that we live in, coding is simply invaluable. It has the power to uplift your career, your future prospects, and even your intellectual capacity. Computation is driving one of the largest capital expansions in history, and there has never been a better time to learn coding than now.

Why Learn Coding?

My first serious interaction with coding was at college. We had to take a course on a programming language called C Sharp. I failed the course the first time I had to take it and barely passed it the second time when I had to take it again. With that defeat in mind, I stayed away from coding for the longest time. I considered it to be a talent that I simply didn't possess. Later, I went on to change my career from engineering to visual effects as I wanted to work in a field that had more room for creative expression. But working in visual effects, I came to realize that the entire operation is actually enabled by the power of computation. From the software that is used to the pipeline management that facilitates the production... Coding is everywhere. It allows studios to deliver mind-blowing effects for movies that make hundreds of millions of dollars in the box office.

Upon realizing the power of coding in my field, I decided to embark on a journey to learn more about it. I ended up teaching myself Python, a programming language that is widely used in visual effects. And doing

© Engin Arslan 2018
E. Arslan, *Learn JavaScript with p5.js*, https://doi.org/10.1007/978-1-4842-3426-6_1

so has been immensely gratifying. Not only has it allowed me to become more accomplished in my work in visual effects and create award-winning effects, but it has also empowered me to transition to an even more rewarding career in software development.

Coding vs. Programming

You must be hearing the terms coding and programming in similar contexts and might be wondering what the difference between them is. In the past few years, coding has become the term of choice to make programming more approachable to the general population. Basically the premise is that you could be coding and still be contributing to the digital economy without actually doing programming.

Let me give you an example of that: you could be using web languages such as HTML and CSS, which are not programming languages. So when coding in those languages you are not really programming but styling or structuring websites (more on their usage in the next section). But you could also be coding in JavaScript, which is an actual programming language. Programming languages allow you to make a computer "do" things. Every time you are programming something, you are also coding. But when you are coding, you might not be programming. Coding is a more general term that is used for describing all cases where you are communicating intent to the computer.

Basically you can think of programming as a subset of coding. But if truth be told, these two terms are used almost interchangeably nowadays. The main purpose of this book is to teach you how to program. We will be coding for programming purposes by using the programming language JavaScript.

On HTML and CSS

Looking at my path for learning programming, I find some of the efforts to teach coding to beginners to be a bit lacking. One of the primary problems in the area is using HTML and CSS as introductory languages.

The problem with these languages is that they are not even programming languages! HTML is a markup language that is used to define the structure of a document in a way that a web browser would understand. For example, HTML teaches you how to write text for a browser so that the browser would know what parts of it is a document header vs. a paragraph, etc...

Likewise, CSS is not a programming language either. It is a styling language that allows us to style HTML documents to have them look aesthetically pleasing and ideally make them more user friendly than before. Furthermore, even though CSS can be used to create incredibly good looking results, it is usually very unintuitive to work with and can be hard to reason about even for a programmer. Learning CSS, you are not only not learning programming, you are very likely engaging in an activity that might not be fun as a beginner if styling websites is not your sole intention.

This push to teach coding using these languages is understandable. After all, given the large dominance of web applications and their immense profitability in certain cases, people found themselves wanting to build their own projects for the Web. And if you are to build a website, you need to use these languages to a certain degree. But having these languages as a starting point could create a misconception about what coding is. Coding can be an immensely rewarding and engaging activity when you are building programs or applications as the domain of possibilities is substantially bigger. As discussed previously, we need to be using programming languages to build programs so the apparent question is: "What makes a language a programming language?"

You can always check Wikipedia for a semi-formal definition. But to me, for a language to be considered a programming language, it needs to have certain control structures available to it that would allow us to express some basic operations. Even this definition probably makes little sense to a beginner. What is meant is that there are structures in programming languages that allow the computer to perform *logical* operations. Some of the examples of such structures, which we will see more about later, are the following: conditionals that allow the program to output different results based on given conditions and variables that store values or loops that allow a program to repeat operations for a desired amount of time. Don't worry if none of this makes any sense right now; the purpose of this book is for us to learn about all these fundamental programming concepts.

Almost all programming languages have these kinds of basic structures that enable us to construct immensely more complicated applications. Think of English, or any other language you might know. You have verbs, nouns, and adjectives. And using these building blocks, people can say the simplest things or go on to write amazing novels. And these are the building blocks that are missing from HTML and CSS that make people miss out on what could be achieved when using programming languages.

In this book we will learn all these basic structures that would allow us to communicate our intent to the computer using the programming language JavaScript.

Why Learn JavaScript?

There are many programming languages out there. This book will be teaching you how to code, by using the immensely popular programming language JavaScript.

JavaScript is one of the most widely used programming languages out there as it is built into every web browser. Due to this, almost all the web pages and applications out there use JavaScript to some degree. In recent years JavaScript started to be used not only to program user interaction in web pages but also server side - back-end - applications, Internet of Things (IOT) devices or mobile apps for platforms such as Android or iPhone. Even though it has its roots in web development, JavaScript knowledge is now applicable to a vast number of other domains.

Given the popularity and ubiquity of JavaScript, it is really easy to find resources and information about it if you are to ever get stuck. It has a big, vibrant community behind it. In the popular Q&A website, StackOverflow, there are more than a million questions that are related to JavaScript. If you end up coding in this language and get stuck in a problem, the chances are that someone else also had the same problem, posted a question on this website, and got an answer that you can learn from.

I won't go into details of what makes a programming language dynamic or static, but being a dynamic programming language, JavaScript code is more concise and easier to write compared to static languages. Listings 1-1 and 1-2 are some examples where a simple statement that displays the words 'hello world' to the screen are written by using different languages. Notice how much shorter it is to write the same code using JavaScript.

Listing 1-1. Displaying Hello World to the screen in C++ (Source: http://helloworldcollection.de/)

```
// Hello World in C++ (pre-ISO)
#include <iostream.h>

main()
{
        cout << "Hello World!" << endl;
        return 0;
}
```

Listing 1-2. Displaying Hello World to the screen in Java (Source: http://helloworldcollection.de/)

```
// Hello World in Java

class HelloWorld {
        static public void main( String args[] ) {
                System.out.println( "Hello World!" );
        }
}
```

Displaying Hello World to the screen in JavaScript:

```
console.log('Hello World');
```

One other advantage of learning JavaScript is that, since it is the language of the Web, you would be able to share your creations with other people in a really easy manner. I think to be able to do so and receive feedback is an important consideration when learning a new skill set.

To summarize, there are lots of reasons to learn programming and JavaScript stands to be a great choice since it:

- is easier to write;

- is popular and ubiquitous;

- has a vast application domain.

Why Do We Have Different Languages?

You must be wondering why there are different languages if they are all share similar features.

That's a great question. Different languages exist because they are designed with different principles in mind. Some of them can be harder to type out, but they give you more control over the stability and speed of your programs. Others can be much more concise but could be slower to execute. Some languages are better suited for certain tasks. JavaScript is perfect for full stack web development, Matlab is great for mathematical calculations, C++ has dominance in game programming, and Julia is used for data science. This doesn't mean you can't be using other languages in these domains, though. Unity Game Engine offers C# for game development. Python can be preferred for data science. And GoLang or many other languages could be used for back-end web development. It sometimes boils down to what the developers prefer to use and what they already know. And sometimes it comes down to the constraints of a given project.

I used to work in the visual effects industry and the software packages that we would be using in the field could be automated using Python or C++. So those were great language choices for that domain given that's what the tools that we were using were supporting. Knowing Java in visual effects would have been largely useless except for the fact that knowing a programming language actually makes it more likely that you will be able to pick up another language as they share similar principles among each other.

Choosing which language to learn as your first can sometimes be a tough choice as there are lots of viable options out there. Sometimes the choice is dictated by the application domain. If you are seeking to build a game using the Unreal Engine maybe you should just learn C++. But then again if it's your first time interfacing with a programming language, you might be faced with such a steep learning curve that it might be discouraging.

JavaScript stands to be a great choice to learn as your first programming language. As mentioned earlier, it is widely used and has a vast application domain that would allow you to experiment with lots of different applications. It has a big and active community behind it and also has a very concise syntax that makes it closer to human languages.

Learning JavaScript with p5.js

One of the most challenging aspects of learning programming is to find engaging examples that are not only fun and impressive but also illustrative of the subject matter at hand. Once you get the hang of it, programming is a highly rewarding and engaging activity, but to a beginner most of the problems that a professional programmer has to tackle might seem uninteresting or straight up boring. That's why this book uses a JavaScript library, an add-on, called p5.js in teaching this introduction to programming book. p5.js will allow you to create engaging interactive and visual pieces that you will have fun while creating, and it will also let you build a strong foundation for software development. The visual nature of this library will allow us to actually see the results from our scripts as graphics and develop an intimate understanding of programming structures.

p5.js is a programming library. A programming library can be thought as a collection of code that is built for a specific purpose, so that whenever you need to perform an action that relates to that purpose you can use a library instead of building that functionality yourself. Libraries build on and extend the core capabilities of a language. For JavaScript, there are more than a hundred thousand libraries out there that allow you to perform a large variety of operations. So it is always a good idea to check if someone already created an open source or even a paid library for your needs before trying to implement your own functionality. The idea is that a library would be a battle-tested solution for a particular problem that you can utilize with confidence, instead of devising your own solution, which might introduce unforeseen problems into the program you are developing. This is particularly true for JavaScript as the core language doesn't have any built-in, standard, library; and hence development efforts rely heavily on external libraries to tackle common problems. Here are examples for a couple of interesting libraries to give you a taste of what is available out there:

- Faker.js (`https://github.com/Marak/Faker.js`): Generate massive amounts of fake data.

- franc (`https://github.com/wooorm/franc`): Detect the language of a given text.

- jimp (`https://github.com/oliver-moran/jimp`): An image processing library.

- cylon.js (`https://cylonjs.com/`): A robotics framework for robotics, physical computing and the Internet of Things.

p5.js is a creative coding library that is based on the idea of sketching. Just like how sketching can be thought of as a minimal approach to drawing to quickly prototype an idea, p5.js is built on the concept of writing the minimal amount of code to translate your visual, interaction, or animation ideas to the screen. p5.js is a JavaScript implementation of the popular library called Processing, which is based on the Java programming language.

It is worth mentioning that Java and JavaScript are completely unrelated languages. The reason why JavaScript is named after Java is an unfortunate branding and marketing decision made back in the day.

The concise nature of p5.js makes it a very easy library to learn. But don't let this simplicity trick you into believing that p5.js has limited capabilities. p5.js has an impressive amount of functionality, history, and community behind it to make it a valuable learning investment if you ever wanted to create art, design, motion, or interactive pieces using code. A p5.js program can be anywhere from a few lines of code to thousands. Since p5.js was built with simplicity in mind, sometimes small p5.js programs are referred to as sketches. Even though that's a clever way to describe it, I am personally not a huge fan of that wording since it obfuscates the fact that what you are doing is programming after all.

You can find pragmatic applications of p5.js such as creating data visualizations (Figure 1-1).

Figure 1-1. *Data visualization with p5.js*

Or you can use it to create abstract generative art (Figure 1-2).

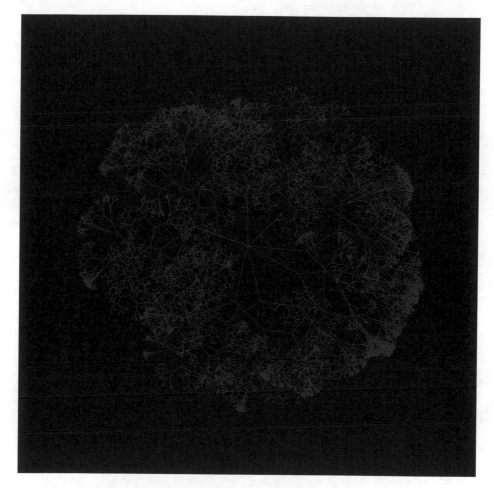

Figure 1-2. *Abstract generative art with p5.js*

You can even create animated or interactive visuals. We will be building an interactive game by the end of this book using p5.js!

CHAPTER 2

Getting Started

Installing p5.js

There are a couple of ways you can start using p5.js and JavaScript. One option is to visit the p5.js website (`https://p5js.org/download`) and download the p5.js source code on to your system (see Figure 2-1).

At the time of the writing of this walkthrough, the download page has a link called 'p5.js complete' that includes the p5.js library and an example project. Download this archive file and find the folder named `empty-example` inside it. In this folder, you will find two files: the `sketch.js` file where you can write JavaScript code and an `index.html` file that can be launched with a web browser such as Chrome and would execute and display the result of the JavaScript code inside `sketch.js` file. You can also find a copy of these files on my GitHub repository: `https://github.com/hibernationTheory/p5js-complete`.

Even though you can change the contents of `sketch.js` JavaScript file with a plain text editor like *NotePad*, you might instead want to use a code editor such as `Sublime Text` to do so.

A code editor is pretty similar to a text editor, like *Notepad* or *Word*, but it has special features that make coding much easier such as highlighting of special words for a given programming language, which in this case that language is JavaScript. Sublime Text is a code editor that you can use, which can be downloaded and evaluated for free.

© Engin Arslan 2018
E. Arslan, *Learn JavaScript with p5.js*, https://doi.org/10.1007/978-1-4842-3426-6_2

Perhaps the easiest way to get started with p5.js is to use an online editor. An online code editor can be used inside the web browser and doesn't require you to install anything on your system. It is my preferred way of working when I am learning as it makes it really easy to get started.

An easy-to-use Online Code Editor that is available at the time of the preparation of this book can be found at this link:

[p5.js online editor - alpha](`https://alpha.editor.p5js.org/`)

If the above link is not accessible for any reason, you can also try the p5.js template that is hosted on my Codepen account:

[Codepen - p5.js simple template](`https://codepen.io/ enginarslan/pen/qpBBXz?editors=0011`). CodePen (`https://codepen. io`) is a social development platform that allows you to write code in the browser and share your work with other developers. It is a great environment for development and experimentation. The difference between Codepen and the p5.js editor that is mentioned above is that the p5.js editor only allows you to run p5.js related code inside itself whereas Codepen can execute any front-end code.

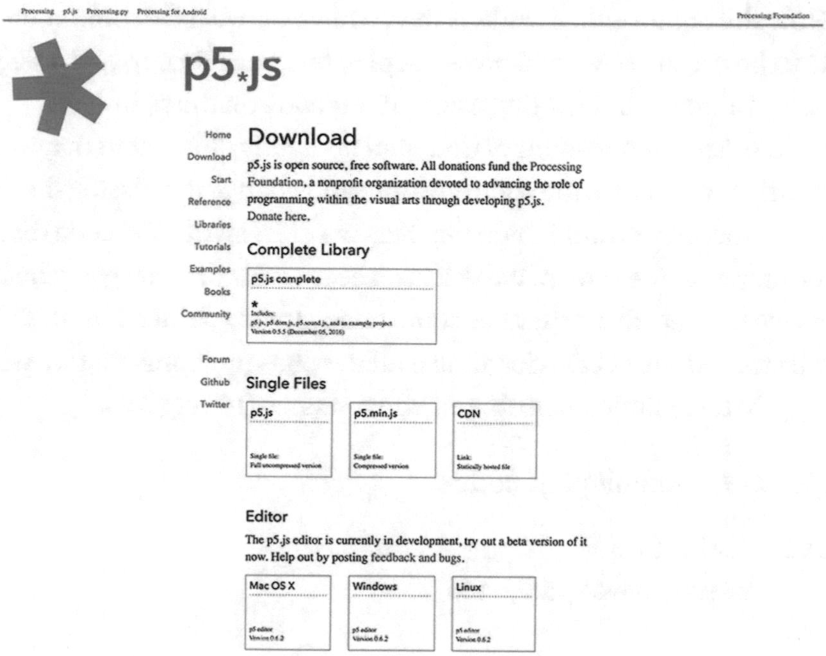

Figure 2-1. *Web page to download p5.js source code*

Figure 2-2. *p5.js online editor*

How the online editor works is that, whenever we have some code ready to be executed, we will press the play button at the top of the page. This play button will show the results of our code on the right-hand side panel. The online editor of Codepen is slightly different in that it automatically executes the code any time you change it. Pressing the Play button at this point wouldn't do much as we didn't write any code that draws shapes to the screen. We will just see an empty screen get generated. But as we can see, this editor has some code already written into it. This code that we see is needed for almost all the p5.js programs that we will be writing so it is included here for our convenience (Listing 2-1).

Listing 2-1. Default p5.js code

```
function setup() {
        createCanvas(400, 400);
}

function draw() {
        background(220);
}
```

Let's just delete this code for now. Before we start using p5.js to learn JavaScript, we will see a couple of things on the fundamentals of JavaScript.

You can find the code examples that we will be using throughout this book at the GitHub repository: https://github.com/hibernationTheory/coding-for-visual-learners.

Gentle Introduction to JavaScript

We can write something as simple as 1 + 1 to the screen. This is a valid JavaScript code that adds these two numbers together. If we are to execute this code by pressing the Play button, we still won't see anything. This is kind of disappointing because we would have at least expected to see the result of this calculation.

To be able to see the results of JavaScript operations on the screen, we can use a function called `console.log()`.

A function is a programming structure that contains other code inside it that is written to perform a specific action. Functions allow us to perform complex operations by just calling them with their defined function name. When we are calling a function – which we can also refer to as *executing* the function – we would write its name, in this case `console.log`, and place brackets next to it. If the function requires an input to perform its functionality, then we would provide that input inside the brackets just like we are doing in this example.

`console.log` is a built-in JavaScript function that displays – or logs – the given value inside the console below the editor. When I say built-in, it means that most JavaScript execution environments would have this function. For example, web browsers have a section in their interfaces called `console`, which we can access through the developer tools. p5.js, and Codepen online editors also have a section that is called `console` as well below the editing area.

We can also have user-defined functions that we can create for ourselves that won't be available to anyone else until we somehow share it with other people. Libraries such as p5.js have a bunch of functions of their own. We will be using p5.js functions to draw shapes to the screen and create all kinds of interactive and animated visuals. We will dive more into the concept of functions later on but for now, know that there is this function that comes with JavaScript called `console.log` that accepts a value and displays that value inside the console underneath the editor. Initially the other functions we will learn won't have a dot in their name. `console.log` is a bit different in that sense, but the reasons for the *dot* usage will be explained later.

Let's add a couple of more `console.log` statements into our code (Listing 2-2).

Listing 2-2. `console.log` statements

```
console.log(1 + 1)
console.log(5 + 10)
console.log(213 * 63)
console.log(321314543265 + 342516463155)
```

Listing 2-3 shows the results that will be displayed inside the console once the code in Listing 2-2 is executed.

Listing 2-3. Results for `console.log` statements

```
2
15
13419
663831006420
```

One takeaway should be that code executes from top to bottom. There are some programming structures that alter this flow, but we will see them later on. Another takeaway should be that computers don't mind working with large numbers. We can throw hard operations at them that would take days for a human to perform.

In the last `console.log` statement from Listing 2-2 we have two ridiculously large numbers. What if we wanted to use the resulting number from that operation and subtract 10 from it on the next line? Right now to be able to do this we have to type that number again:

```
console.log(321314543265 + 342516463155 - 10)
```

This is obviously very wasteful. But luckily another thing that computers are great at is storing and remembering values. Therefore we can create something called a `variable` to hold on to that value. In programming languages, a variable is a name that refers to a value.

So we can use a variable name to refer to that value instead of typing the value again. Here is how that works:

```
var bigNumber = 321314543265 + 342516463155
console.log(bigNumber)
console.log(bigNumber - 10)
```

We are creating a variable called bigNumber by using the var keyword. var is the keyword that we need to use whenever we are creating a variable. After the var keyword, we are giving this variable a name, which in this case is bigNumber.

It is important to choose a variable name that makes sense for the current context. In this example, this might not matter too much, but as our programs get more complex, meaningful variable names can help us understand what's going when reading our code. So naming this kind of a variable that holds a large number as cat wouldn't make much sense and can confuse other people that might read our code. It might even confuse us if we are to come back to our code a couple of months later. Programmers always strive to make their code as readable as possible.

Once this variable is declared, we can assign a value to it by using the equal operator. This might seem unusual at first. In Math, the equal operator is used to signify equality in between two values. Here we are using it to do a value assignment to a variable. It takes the value on the right-hand side of the operation and assigns it to the variable on the left-hand side. This is a pretty common procedure that exists in many programming languages.

Now that we have a variable that points to a value, we can use this variable name in operations instead of the value itself. As mentioned earlier, it is good to have variable names that make sense. There are also some rules that govern what we can and can't use as variable names. For example, we can't use some of the special characters such as dashes or exclamation marks or use a space character inside our variable names. Another restriction is that we can't use certain JavaScript reserved names as variable names; we can't call our variable var as this name is already in use by JavaScript. If we tried to use var as a variable name; as in var var = 5, JavaScript would throw an error.

This mention of rules might be making you uneasy at this point. After all, programming is supposed to be fun right? But don't worry; the reserved name list is relatively short, so you don't need to memorize it. And as you learn more of the language, you would also develop a better sense as to which names to avoid.

Regarding rules, there is another rule that should be mentioned. JavaScript needs us to place semicolons after each statement. If we don't do this, our program can still work but might fail in certain edge conditions that can be hard to identify later on. So it is a good idea to use semicolons after every statement even though it means a bit more work on our part. Previous code should actually be written as shown in Listing 2-4:

Listing 2-4. Using semicolons

```
console.log(1 + 1);
console.log(5 + 10);
console.log(213 * 63);
var bigNumber = 321314543265 + 342516463155;
console.log(bigNumber);
console.log(bigNumber - 10);
```

Notice that doing bigNumber - 10 wouldn't change the initial value of the bigNumber variable. In this following example, the console.log statement would still output 10.

```
var x = 10;
x + 5;
console.log(x);
```

If we want to change the value of a variable, then we need to assign a new value to it (Listing 2-5).

Listing 2-5. Overriding the variable value

```
var bigNumber = 321314543265 + 342516463155;
console.log(bigNumber);
bigNumber = 3;
console.log(bigNumber);
```

In this example, the `console.log` would display the value 3 because we override the initial value with another value on line 3.

There is this concept of data types in JavaScript (and in other languages as well) to differentiate between different kinds of values. These numbers that we have been using are of a data type called `Number`. There is another data type called `String` that is used to represent textual information.

In JavaScript, we can't just write a word and expect it to represent data. For example, we want to `console.log` the word `hello`. If we do this right now, we will notice that we are getting an error. JavaScript doesn't understand what `hello` means. It assumes that it is a variable that is not defined yet.

```
console.log(hello);
> 1: Uncaught ReferenceError: hello is not defined
```

But what if we wanted to actually input the word `hello` to the computer? There are programs out there that work with textual data, which needs to process a given name or address, etc. In that case we can provide the data using quotation marks, which means that we are providing the value as a `string`.

```
console.log('hello');
```

JavaScript is not complaining this time. Anytime we are dealing with textual data, we need to place it in quotation marks; this would make it registered as a `string`. And when I say textual data, it can be numbers as well. A `string` can consist of numeric values:

```
console.log('1234');
```

In that case, they are not treated as Mathematical numbers that we can perform Math operations with, but just as text.

We can perform operations on strings, but it doesn't yield the same result as when we would perform those operations using numbers. We can actually add two strings together:

```
console.log('hello' + 'world');
> 'helloworld'
```

And this will just combine these two words together. And when I say we can't perform Math operations with strings that contain numeric values, this is what it meant:

```
console.log('1' + '1');
> '11'
```

In this case, the numeric values are not treated as numbers but as strings, and they are not summed together but combined. This act of combining strings is commonly referred to as concatenation operation in programming.

String might sound like a weird name choice, but it refers to *string of characters*. So a string is actually a collection of individual characters as far as the computer is concerned. We can define strings by using either a single quotation ' or double quotation marks " but we have to finish the string with the same symbol we choose to start defining with. Also in our programs, we shouldn't use one type of quotation mark for one string and another for a different one. Consistency is very important when developing programs.

One other thing that's worth mentioning before wrapping up this section is the concept of comments. Comments allow us to write things into our programs that won't get executed by the computer, as shown in Listing 2-6.

Listing 2-6. Example for using comments in our program

```
// various examples. (this is a comment)
console.log(1 + 1);
console.log(5 + 10);
console.log(213 * 63);
var bigNumber = 321314543265 + 342516463155;
console.log(bigNumber);
console.log(bigNumber - 10);
```

The line that starts with double slashes // gets ignored by JavaScript. Double slashes allow us to comment on a single line; if we needed to comment on multiple lines, we would either need to use double slashes at the beginning of each line or use the /* */ symbol, as shown in Listing 2-7.

Listing 2-7. Using // and /* */ for comments

```
// various examples
// disabling the first 3 lines by using multiline comments:
/*
console.log(1 + 1);
console.log(5 + 10);
console.log(213 * 63);
*/
var bigNumber = 321314543265 + 342516463155;
console.log(bigNumber);
console.log(bigNumber - 10);
```

Believe it or not, this is enough of a JavaScript primer to get us started with using p5.js. If you are using the code editor, click on the New Project button to be able to get a new editor window that has the template that we will use for our p5.js code.

Getting Started with p5.js

What we see when we start a new project in the p5.js code editor are two function declarations with these names: setup and draw (Listing 2-8).

Listing 2-8. Default function declarations

```
function setup() {

}

function draw() {

}
```

These two function declarations need to be made for pretty much every p5.js program that we would write. p5.js finds these function definitions in our code and executes whatever is written inside them. But there is a difference in between how these functions are executed.

The block inside the setup function, the area in between the curly brackets, is the place where we will be writing the code that is to be executed for the initialization of our program. Code written inside the setup function is executed only once before the draw function.

```
function setup() {
        // write your code for setup function inside these
        curly brackets
}
```

The draw function is where the real magic happens. Any code that is written inside the draw function is repeatedly executed by p5.js. This allows us to create all sorts of animated and interactive works.

p5.js makes sure to execute the setup function before the draw function. And to reiterate, p5.js executes the setup function only once but the draw function over and over again (actually close to 60 times a second). And this is how we can create interactive and animated content using p5.js.

We can actually see this in action by placing console.log statements at different places in our code. Place a console.log() statement inside the setup function, inside the draw function, and outside both of these functions using different values (Listing 2-9).

Listing 2-9. Logging the behavior of setup and draw functions.

```
function setup() {
        console.log('setup');
}

function draw() {
        console.log('draw');
}

console.log('hello');
```

Let's execute this code and immediately try to stop it. We would notice that the message hello is displayed as the very first thing. This is an expected behavior. A function call that we have should be executed by JavaScript. What is rather unexpected is that setup and draw functions get executed as well. This is unexpected because these are only function declarations; they define the behavior of a function, but we still need to execute these functions to be able to use them.

This means that if we were just using JavaScript, we would need to call the setup and draw functions explicitly in order to have the console.log messages inside them to be displayed:

```
setup();
draw();
console.log('hello');
```

But we don't need to do this using the p5.js library. Because of how the p5.js library is architected, it looks for function declarations with the name setup and draw and executes these functions for us. The reason why p5.js takes control of the execution of these functions is that it executes them in a very specific manner.

p5.js executes the `setup` function only once and then goes on to execute the draw function in a repeated manner such that if we don't stop the process, it will just keep working forever. This is a very standard behavior with any graphical interface – think of the web browser, the games you play, or the operating system you interface with. These are just programs that continuously work – and display to the screen – until we explicitly close them. This is why p5.js creates an execution loop for the `draw` function so that things will persist on the screen instead of appearing for a second and then disappearing.

More About Functions

Let's talk more about functions because they will be the building blocks of the programs that we will be writing.

Function names are usually verbs. They represent the specific action that can be performed by executing that function. Hypothetically speaking, we might have a function called `drawCat` that when called can draw a cat to the screen:

```
drawCat();
```

However, this is not hypothetical at all as I actually created a cat drawing function that is called `drawCat` for this chapter (Figure 2-3). We are free to create whatever functions we want to create in JavaScript, and that gives us immense power when programming applications.

Figure 2-3. *The graphic output of the* drawCat *function*

OK, to be fair, this function doesn't do a great job in drawing a cat.

To use a function, we call it by its name and then put parentheses next to it to have the function executed. Sometimes functions, depending on how they are created or defined, are parameterized. This means they can accept input values that would affect the outcome of a function. For example, a drawCat function might get a number input, which would determine the size of the cat that is drawn. Or maybe the number input determines the amount of cats that would be drawn to the screen. It really depends on how this function is constructed.

In our example, this function that I created can get an input that allows us to change the size of the cat head that gets drawn on the screen (Figure 2-4):

```
drawCat(2);
```

Figure 2-4. *Drawing a cat face*

Unfortunately, p5.js doesn't come with a `drawCat` function – I had to create my own – but it has lots of other useful functions that allow us to perform complicated tasks in an easy manner. To be able to do anything using the p5.js library, we will be using the functions that come with it, which are coded by the smart people who created this library.

Here is a function from p5.js library that probably all the sketches we will be writing will require: the `createCanvas` function. What the `createCanvas` function does is that it creates a drawing-area canvas inside the web page for us to work. But for this function to work, we need to provide it with two comma-separated values: a width and height for the drawing area. We should be calling the `createCanvas` function inside the `setup` function because it only needs to get executed once and it needs to be executed before we can do any drawing.

Let's provide this function with the values 800 and 300 and execute our sketch to see what's happening (Listing 2-10). It seems like not much has changed, but the size of the browser window that gets launched seems to have increased. It is now using the dimensions that we have provided. Let's change the dimensions again to see the window size updating.

Listing 2-10. Working with the `createCanvas` function

```
function setup() {
        createCanvas(800, 300);
}

function draw() {
}
```

There is another function that we will frequently be using, which is called background. The background function sets the color of the canvas using the given value. We will look at how color values are represented in p5.js in another chapter, but for now, we can just provide this function with the value (220, 220, 220) to see the background become light gray (Listing 2-11).

Listing 2-11. Working with the `background` function

```
function setup() {
        createCanvas(800, 300);
        background(220,220,220);
}

function draw() {
}
```

As we can see again, the code is executed from top to bottom. p5.js first creates the canvas for us and then sets the background to be gray.

It is worth emphasizing this once more: the setup and draw are function definitions that we need for p5.js to work correctly. Our job when we are using p5.js is to determine what is placed inside these functions that are executed by p5.js. This is due to how p5.js is architected. The creators of p5.js wanted to make sure some of the code we will write will only be executed once for initialization and setup purposes, while some will be executed all the time for drawing, animation, and interactivity purposes.

We used functions that come with the p5.js library such as createCanvas and background inside these function definitions. These functions are already defined by someone else so we don't actually know what code is contained inside them. But we don't really need to have this knowledge anyway since all we care about is what they do and how to use them.

Functions allow us to perform complicated tasks in an easy manner. By using the createCanvas function, we don't need to know what kind of work goes into creating a canvas element in a page. These details are hidden away, abstracted, from us. We just need to know how to call this function to make it work for us.

Finally, we will be calling one more function, this time inside the draw function definition, to draw a rectangle on the page (Listing 2-12).

To draw a rectangle we will be utilizing a function called rect. The rect function requires us to provide it with four input values: the x and y position of the upper-left corner of the rectangle inside the canvas drawing area, and the width and height values for the rectangle.

Without knowing anything about how the coordinates work in p5.js, we will just provide this function with the x value of 50, y of 100, the width of 200, and height of 100 (Figure 2-5).

Listing 2-12. Drawing a rectangle

```
function setup() {
        createCanvas(800, 300);
        background(220,220,220);
}

function draw() {
        rect(50, 100, 200, 100);
}
```

Figure 2-5. *Output of the rect function*

By calling this function, we drew our first shape to the screen!

Coordinates in p5.js

At this point, let's take some time to explain how the coordinate system works in p5.js.

To locate any point on a flat surface, we use a two-axis coordinate system. The vertical axis is called the Y-axis, and the horizontal one is the X-axis. The point where these two axes meet is called the origin. In canvas, where we draw our shapes, the origin point is at the top left of the canvas. From there below, the Y values increases; and to the right, the X values increases (Figure 2-6).

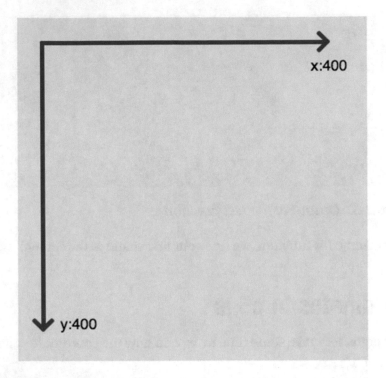

Figure 2-6. *Coordinate origins*

When we draw a rectangle to the screen, provided coordinates define the top-left corner of the rectangle (Listing 2-13 and Figure 2-7).

Listing 2-13. Drawing a rectangle

```
function setup() {
      createCanvas(800, 300);
      background(220,220,220);
}

function draw() {
      rect(400, 150, 100, 100);
}
```

Figure 2-7. *Drawing a rectangle*

If this is not the behavior that you want, we can make a call to another p5.js function called rectMode and provide it with the value CENTER to change how rectangles are drawn in our program (Listing 2-14). Since this function is more like a setup and initialization-related function, we will be placing it under the setup function definition.

Listing 2-14. Using the rectMode function and CENTER value

```
function setup() {
        createCanvas(800, 300);
        background(220,220,220);
        rectMode(CENTER);
}

function draw() {
        rect(400, 150, 100, 100);
}
```

Figure 2-8. *Output for a centered rectangle*

There is also an ellipse function in p5.js to draw circular shapes. How ellipse works is very similar to the rect function. First, two arguments are x and y coordinates of the center of the ellipse, the third argument is the horizontal radius, and the fourth one is the vertical radius. So to be able to draw a circle with the ellipse function, we need to provide equal horizontal and vertical radius values for it (Listing 2-15).

If you are experimenting with drawing these shapes to the screen, you might have noticed at this point that, whenever a shape function is called, it draws itself on top of the previous shapes. We can change the order of the function calls to affect the stacking order of the shapes.

Listing 2-15. Using the ellipse function

```
function setup() {
        createCanvas(800, 300);
        background(220,220,220);
        rectMode(CENTER);
}

function draw() {
        rect(400, 150, 100, 100);
        ellipse(350, 120, 100, 100);
}
```

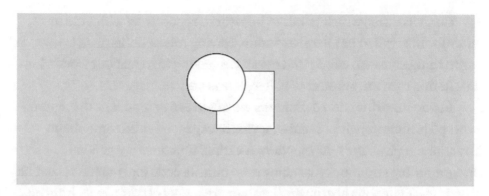

Figure 2-9. *Output for an ellipse and centered rectangle*

One more drawing function that I want to introduce is the line function. As the name implies, the line function draws a line to the screen. We need to provide four arguments to the line function: the starting x and y coordinates and the ending x and y coordinates. Play with the line function a bit; it will give you a good sense of how the coordinate system works in p5.js. You can, for example, try drawing an X that spans the entire canvas.

Summary

In this chapter we made a quick start with using p5.js and actually drew shapes on the screen.

We have seen that we need to write our code in two function definition blocks that go with the name setup and draw. Anything that only needs to be executed once is placed under the setup function, and anything that we might like to animate or interact with goes into the draw function. Writing our code into these two functions is something that p5.js requires us to do. It is not a general programming principle, convention, or anything like that. We could have been using a different library that doesn't require this kind of a structuring to our code. This requirement has to do with how p5.js is architected as a library. We will need to start all of our p5.js sketches with these two function definitions.

Code like this, which needs to be written repetitively with little or no alteration, is called `boilerplate` code. Having lots of boilerplate is never a good thing since we would find ourselves having to repeat our work a lot, but in this case the amount of boilerplate is very manageable.

Inside these function definitions we made use of functions that come with p5.js library such as `createCanvas`, `background,` and some shape functions such as `rect`. As mentioned earlier, functions are general programming structures that allow us to bundle code together for reusability purposes. Functions also abstract away a great deal of complexity from us. We don't need to know how a function works; we just need to know how to use it. We can absolutely have no idea how the `createCanvas` actually creates a canvas element inside a web page. It doesn't matter as long as we know how to use this function. Think of driving a car; we don't necessarily need to know how an internal combustion engine works to be able to drive it. We just need to know how to interface with the car using the steering wheel, the pedals, etc. This similar idea applies to the functions as well.

Later on, we will be creating our functions as well to manage the complexity of our programs and to create reusable pieces of code.

Practice

Try to re-create the image in Figure 2-10.

Figure 2-10. *Practice image*

CHAPTER 3

Colors in p5.js

Now that we can draw shapes in p5.js, let's look at how to control the color in our sketches. We are already assigning a light gray color to the background by passing the values 220, 220, 220 to the background function.

Color Functions in p5.js

p5.js by default uses the RGB color system where R stands for red, G stands for green, and B stands for blue. This means that we will *usually* need to pass these three color components to a color accepting function to set the desired color. Each of these color components can have a value in between 0 and 255. This means that if we are to pass 0, 0, 0 to the background function, we will end up getting a black color for the background and if we are to pass 255, 255, 255, we will get a white color. p5.js, being a helpful library, allows us to pass a single value when we want all these three values to be equal. This means that instead of passing 0, 0, 0; we can also just pass a single 0.

Whenever we have equal amounts of these three color components, the resulting color will be a white, black, or a shade of gray. So passing a single value to a color setting function is useful if we wanted to have a grayscale color. But if we want hue in our color, then we need to pass all these three values to be able to specify the amount that we want for each component. The number 255 is the maximum value that a color

© Engin Arslan 2018
E. Arslan, *Learn JavaScript with p5.js*, https://doi.org/10.1007/978-1-4842-3426-6_3

component can accept; so if we are to pass 255, 0, 0 as a color to the background function we will get a pure red color. If we pass 0, 255, 0, then we will get a pure green color, and so on.

The RGB color model is an additive model, which means that adding these colors together in their full intensity will result in white compared to paint colors that are subtractive, where adding them all together will result in a dark-brownish color. Finding the exact color that you want by tinkering with these values can be a bit hard if you are not too familiar working with additive RGB colors. If that's the case you can use an online color picker service to help you with finding the desired color. An online search for the term "color picker" will result in numerous results that you can use to identify the RGB components for the desired color. Here is an example service from Firefox (Figure 3-1).

- Color picker tool: https://developer.mozilla.org/
  en-US/docs/Web/CSS/CSS_Colors/Color_picker_tool

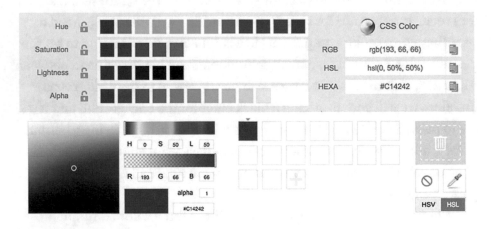

Figure 3-1. *Firefox color picker tool*

Using a service like this, you can make note of the RGB values that correspond to the color that you choose and make use of those values inside p5.js.

We can actually pass a fourth argument to a color setting function. This fourth argument, called the alpha component of the color, controls the opacity of the color and again accepts values from 0 to 255. A 0 would result in full transparency and 255 would result in full opaqueness.

So we can pass a single value, three values, or four values to a color setting function. I don't want to overwhelm you with too much information, but we can pass only two arguments as well. If we are to do so, we would be setting a grayscale color and an alpha component for that grayscale color.

If this abundance of options seems overwhelming, remember that they are there for our convenience. p5.js could have restricted the color functions to only work with four inputs, which would have covered all the cases but would have been time consuming to provide additional data when we only wanted something like opaque white, which happens more often than not. It seems like developers of p5.js built their functions smart enough so that they would result in different output based on a different number of arguments.

Changing Shape Colors

Knowing how the colors work in p5.js is great, but we can only change the color of the background so far. To be able to change the color of the shapes, we will have to make use of a couple of more functions.

The first function that we should know of is fill. fill allows us to set the fill color of the shapes. Fill color is the color that fills inside the shapes and if you are wondering what other color controls there are for shapes, there is also the stroke color that defines the color of the outline of a shape. The default color for the fill and the stroke is white and black respectively. All the shapes except for line have both a fill and a stroke color.

We can set the fill color of the shapes by calling the fill function and passing color arguments to this function as discussed earlier. The fill function will set the active color to be the chosen color until we set the color to something else by using another fill function.

The stroke function works in a similar manner. We pass it color arguments, and it sets the color of the stroke for all the shapes until the next stroke function. A fill or a stroke function that comes after a prior one would override the settings of those prior.

At this point, one other useful function to know could be strokeWeight, which allows us to set the thickness of an outline.

Listing 3-1 is a small sketch that makes use of some of the functions we learned about in this chapter. You can see the results of Listing 3-1 in Figure 3-2.

Listing 3-1. Using fill, stroke, and strokeWeight functions

```
function setup() {
        createCanvas(800, 400);
}

function draw() {
        background(220);

        // circle 01
        fill(51, 51, 51);
        strokeWeight(2);
        stroke(75);
        ellipse(400, 200, 300, 300);

        // circle 02
        stroke(0);
        fill(255, 53, 139);
        ellipse(400, 200, 275, 275);
```

```
// circle 03
fill(1, 176, 240);
ellipse(400, 200, 250, 250);

// circle 04
fill(174, 238, 0);
ellipse(400, 200, 150, 150);
}
```

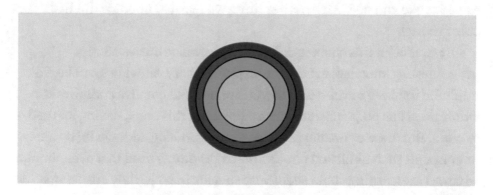

Figure 3-2. *Output showing the use of fill, stroke, and strokeWeight functions*

Notice how we are using the fill function before the shape that I want to set the color for. And we keep using it to be able to switch the color for different ellipses.

Two more functions that are worth mentioning are noFill and noStroke functions. As their name implies, when called, these functions will respectively get rid of the fill and the stroke of shapes. These functions are called without any arguments.

```
noFill();
noStroke();
```

Summary

In this chapter, we haven't seen any new JavaScript functionalities or new programming structures. We just looked at some operating principles of the p5.js library and some specific functions that come with it. In particular, we learned about how some of the color-setting functions work in p5.js, such as `fill`, `stroke`, and `strokeWeight`. We also learned about other functions that are related to fill and stroke operations such as `noStroke` and `noFill`. Another thing we learned about is the RGB color model.

Even though this chapter didn't really advance our JavaScript programming knowledge, I think one point is very valuable to make. You might be thinking to yourself that you are not into creative coding and won't need this p5.js specific information after this book, having learned to code. But these operating principles such as using additive RGB values, or concepts such as fill and stroke are so commonly used that even though what we are learning could seem very specific to p5.js, they are general principles or concepts that are utilized by lots of other drawing libraries or programs. Understanding them will serve us well in our journey of learning how to program.

Practice

Build the script in Listing 3-1 in such a way that one variable would control the size of all the circles (meaning changing that variable should change the size of all the circles) and another one should control the radius difference for all the circles (results in Figure 3-3 and Figure 3-4).

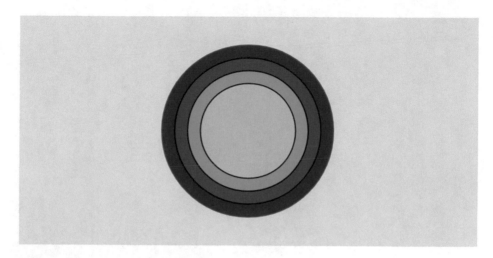

Figure 3-3. *Practice image*

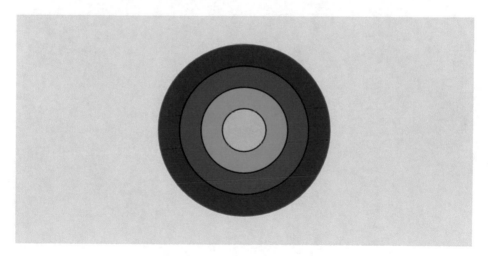

Figure 3-4. *Practice Image - 2*

CHAPTER 4

Operators and Variables

In Chapters 1 and 2 we learned about variables and math operations that we can use in JavaScript. In this chapter, we will put that knowledge to use.

Setup

Let's first create a couple of shapes to have something to work with. Using the `ellipse` and `rect` functions, let's create a shape that roughly resembles a cart (Listing 4-1 and Figure 4-1).

Listing 4-1. Creating a cart using `rect` and `ellipse` functions

```
function setup() {
        createCanvas(800, 300);
}

function draw() {
        background(220);

        ellipse(100, 200, 50, 50); // left wheel
        ellipse(200, 200, 50, 50); // right wheel
        rect(50, 160, 200, 20) // cart
}
```

© Engin Arslan 2018
E. Arslan, *Learn JavaScript with p5.js*, https://doi.org/10.1007/978-1-4842-3426-6_4

Figure 4-1. *Output of Listing 4-1*

Looking at our rough drawing in Figure 4-1, I am not entirely happy with its position. I now wish that we drew it more to the right-hand side. Moving the shape now will mean that we would need to increase the value of the x position argument of each of the shape functions.

Let's assume that we want to add 150 to all these numbers that specify the x position. We can try to do the math in our head and type the result in there, but luckily we can do math operations easily with JavaScript. Instead of typing the result of addition, we can just type out the operation needed, and JavaScript will do the calculation for us (Listing 4-2 and Figure 4-2).

Listing 4-2. Using Math Operations

```
function setup() {
      createCanvas(800, 300);
}

function draw() {
      background(220);

      ellipse(100 + 150, 200, 50, 50);
      ellipse(200 + 150, 200, 50, 50);
      rect(50 + 150, 160, 200, 20)
}
```

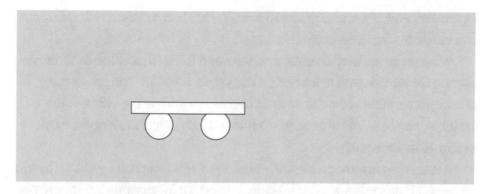

Figure 4-2. *Output of Listing 4-2*

The same thing works with other operators as well; we can do subtraction, multiplication, or division in a similar manner.

One thing that we need to keep in mind with operators is the order of operations. You might already know this from your math classes, but some operators take precedence over others. For example, if we wanted to add 2 to a number and then multiply it by 4, we might be tempted to write something like this: 10 + 2 * 4

But in this operation multiplication will happen before addition. The 2 will get multiplied with 4 before being added to 10, so this above operation will yield 18 instead of the expected value 48.

To be able to control the order of operations we can use parentheses. For example, we can write the top equation like this: (10 + 2) * 4

Anything inside parentheses will be evaluated before other operations. In the order of operations, parentheses come first, then the multiplication and division, and then addition and subtraction.

Variables

To be able to evaluate expressions like this will make our job easier in doing calculations. But I think the real problem here, in this example, is the need to type the same number at all these three different spots. This is very repetitive, laborious, and prone to errors. This is an instance where usage of a variable would be useful.

Whenever we need a value, and we need to use that value in multiple places, we would want to store that value in a variable. The advantage of using a variable is that, if we ever needed to update the value of the variable, we would only need to do it in a single place. Let's update this example to use a variable.

Remember how to create variables. We would start off by using the var keyword. Using this keyword is really important for reasons that are to be discussed later.

Then we would choose a name for our variable. It is also important to choose a name that makes sense. Calling this variable offset or x might make sense as we would be using it to offset shapes in the x-axis. Using sensible names would help others or even us in understanding our code. We always want our programs to be as readable as possible.

Now that we have a variable that points to a value, we can use this variable in operations instead of the value itself. Doing that, we would only need to change the value of this variable from one spot to see the shapes moving (Listing 4-3).

Listing 4-3. Using variable offset

```
function setup() {
        createCanvas(800, 300);
}

function draw() {
        background(220);

        var offset = 150;

        ellipse(100 + offset, 200, 50, 50);
        ellipse(200 + offset, 200, 50, 50);
        rect(50 + offset, 160, 200, 20)
}
```

Variables Continued

I would like to illustrate another behavior of variables in a different example. Let's just draw a single circle in the middle of the screen and a rectangle in the middle (Listing 4-4 and Figure 4-3).

Listing 4-4. Circle and rectangle

```
function setup() {
        createCanvas(800, 300);
        rectMode(CENTER);
}

function draw() {
        background(1, 186, 240);

        // circle
        fill(237, 34, 93);
        noStroke();
        ellipse(400, 150, 200, 200);

        // rectangle
        fill(255);
        rect(400, 150, 150, 30);
}
```

Figure 4-3. *Output from Listing 4-4*

Can you think of one optimization that we could do to the above program? Notice how we are repeating the x and y position values for the shapes. Let's use a variable instead (Listing 4-5).

Listing 4-5. Using a variable to create a circle and rectangle

```
function setup() {
        createCanvas(800, 300);
        rectMode(CENTER);
}

function draw() {
        background(1, 186, 240);

        // declaration of variables
        var x = 400;
        var y = 150;

        // circle
        fill(237, 34, 93);
        noStroke();
        ellipse(x, y, 200, 200);
```

```
    // rectangle
    fill(255);
    rect(x, y, 150, 30);
}
```

Since these shapes are not being positioned relative to the canvas size, if we are to change the size of the canvas, the relative position of the shapes will change as well. For a square canvas, the shape is currently at the center, but for a wider canvas, the shape might start falling to the left-hand side. To have the shapes close to the center for any given canvas size, we can start off by using variables to set the width and height values for the canvas. Then we can utilize the same variables to control the position of the shapes.

Inside the setup function, we are going to create two new variables called canvasWidth and canvasHeight with the value of 800 and 300. And we will pass these variables to the createCanvas function instead of using hard-coded values from before. The plan is that we can use these same variables inside the draw function as well so that even if we are to change the size of the canvas, the relative position of the shapes will remain the same. So let's put these variables into use in the draw function (Listing 4-6). We will divide them by 2 so that we can get the half point of width and height of the canvas.

Listing 4-6. Using variables in the draw function

```
function setup() {
        var canvasWidth = 800;
        var canvasHeight = 300;

        createCanvas(canvasWidth, canvasHeight);
        rectMode(CENTER);
}
```

```
function draw() {
        background(1, 186, 240);

        // declaration of variables
        var x = canvasWidth/2;
        var y = canvasHeight/2;

        // circle
        fill(237, 34, 93);
        noStroke();
        ellipse(x, y, 200, 200);

        // rectangle
        fill(255);
        rect(x, y, 150, 30);
}
```

When executing the code, you will notice that we get an error. If we are to look at the error message inside the console, it says something about the variable name not being defined:

```
Uncaught ReferenceError: canvasHeight is not defined
(sketch: line 14)
Uncaught ReferenceError: canvasWidth is not defined
(sketch: line 14)
```

This might come as a surprise since we clearly declared these variables inside the setup function. The reason for this error has to do with something called the scope. The scope of a variable determines where a variable will be accessible. JavaScript variables have a *function scope* when using the var keyword to declare them.

You can also use the 'let' and 'const' keywords to declare variables as well. Variables that are declared using these keywords have different scoping rules associated with them, but for the purposes of this book we won't be delving into usage of these keywords.

How *function scope* works is that any variable declared inside a function won't be visible from outside the function. It is only available to the function that it lives in and other functions that might be nested inside this function. Likewise, if we were to have a variable that is at the top level, this variable would be visible to everything that is at that level and at levels nested inside, like the functions that might be defined in there. The problem that we are faced with right now is that the variables defined inside the setup function are not visible from the draw function. Therefore if were to declare variables inside the draw function, they wouldn't be visible inside other functions at the same level.

The solution to this problem is this: instead of declaring our variables inside the setup function, we should declare them at this top level so they would be accessible from everything else that is declared inside at the top level (Listing 4-7).

Listing 4-7. Declaring a global variable

```
// declaration of global variables
var canvasWidth = 800;
var canvasHeight = 300;

function setup() {
        createCanvas(canvasWidth, canvasHeight);
        rectMode(CENTER);
}

function draw() {
        background(1, 186, 240);

        // declaration of variables
        var x = canvasWidth/2;
        var y = canvasHeight/2;
```

```
// circle
fill(237, 34, 93);
noStroke();
ellipse(x, y, 200, 200);

// rectangle
fill(255);
rect(x, y, 150, 30);
}
```

A variable that is declared at the top level is called a *global variable.* It is usually not the best idea to declare variables at this top level since we run our code in a browser, where other things that are working in the browser such as plug-ins, add-on's, etc., might cause conflicts by defining variables with the same name for their purposes. Whenever two variable declarations share the same name, the one that gets declared later overwrites the other one since the code is executed from top to bottom. This might result in programs not behaving as expected. But it is not something that you should necessarily worry about as a beginner. Other, more experienced, developers - having the same concern - would have safeguards in place to ensure their variables are not being overwritten. For now, we can put our variables in the top section and be able to share them in different functions that are defined at the same level or below.

In this case, we are initializing the necessary variables outside the setup function so that those variables would be accessible from both the setup and draw functions. Now we can try setting the canvasWidth and canvasHeight variables to different values and notice how the shape always remains at the center because its position is derived using the same variables as the canvas.

Predefined Variables in p5.js

p5.js, being a super helpful library, has a couple of predefined variables that we can use to obtain certain values. Two such variable names that we can use are width and height. By using these variable names inside the setup or draw functions, we can get the current canvas size. This allows us to do the same thing that we were trying to do by defining our own variable names. p5.js developers must have realized this is something that a lot of developers would try to do by themselves and hence provided an easier solution to the problem.

With this knowledge, the code from Listing 4-7 could be written as shown in Listing 4-8.

Listing 4-8. Working with predefined variables

```
function setup() {
        createCanvas(800, 300);
        rectMode(CENTER);
}

function draw() {
        background(1, 186, 240);

        // declaration of variables
        var x = width / 2;
        var y = height / 2;

        // circle
        fill(237, 34, 93);
        noStroke();
        ellipse(x, y, 200, 200);
```

```
    // rectangle
    fill(255);
    rect(x, y, 150, 30);
}
```

You should note that width and height are p5.js variables, which mean that they won't be available outside the setup or draw functions.

Now that we know how to use variables, we can animate our shapes! The trick to animation in p5.js is remembering that the draw function is constantly being executed for us by p5.js. Whatever we are putting inside this function is actually being redrawn each time the draw function is executed again.

The number of times that this draw function is executed (can be thought as rendered to the screen) is called a frame rate. By default, p5.js has a frame rate of 60. This means that it tries to re-draw (or render) the content of the draw function 60 times a second. If we had a way to change the values of the variables that we are using in between each of these draw calls, then we would be able to create animations.

This should remind you of flipbook animations. Each call to a draw function results in a static image, but since it happens 60 times a second when each of these images is slightly different, you perceive it to be animated.

To be able to create an animation, we are going to initialize a variable outside the draw function called count. And inside the draw function, we will use this simple expression that will increment the count variable by one every time the draw function is called.

```
count = count + 1;
```

Now if we are to make use of this variable in a position argument, we can make a shape move (Listing 4-9). This is an amazing step forward in our p5.js adventure.

Listing 4-9. Animating a shape

```
var count = 0; // initialize a counter variable

function setup() {
        createCanvas(800, 300);
        rectMode(CENTER);
}

function draw() {
        background(1, 186, 240);

        // declaration of variables
        var x = width / 2 + count;
        var y = height / 2;

        // circle
        fill(237, 34, 93);
        noStroke();
        ellipse(x, y, 200, 200);

        // rectangle
        fill(255);
        rect(x, y, 150, 30);

        count = count + 1; // increment the counter variable
}
```

What if instead of making the shape move, we wanted to make it bigger? Easy! We will first create a size variable and use that inside our shapes instead of hard-coded values to be able to update the size easier (Listing 4-10).

Listing 4-10. Using a `size` variable

```
var count = 0; // initialize a counter variable

function setup() {
        createCanvas(800, 300);
        rectMode(CENTER);
}

function draw() {
        background(1, 186, 240);

        // declaration of variables
        var x = width / 2;
        var y = height / 2;
        var size = 200 + count; // control the size of the shapes

        // circle
        fill(237, 34, 93);
        noStroke();
        ellipse(x, y, size, size);

        // rectangle
        fill(255);
        rect(x, y, size*0.75, size*0.15);

        count = count + 1; // increment the counter variable
}
```

Summary

In this chapter, we revisited operators that we have seen before and talked a bit about operator precedence. Then we looked at variables again and learned more about their behavior, especially regarding their scope. We also learned about some of the built-in variables that p5.js comes with such as the `width` and `height` that are only available inside the `setup` and `draw` functions.

And finally we created our first animation!

Practice

Create an animation where five rectangles that are initially offscreen are animated to enter the screen from the left-hand side and exit from the right-hand side. They should also be moving at different speeds.

CHAPTER 5

Conditional Statements and Comparison Operators

In the previous chapter, we saw some of the variables that p5.js makes available for us. One important thing to note is that these variables can only be used from inside the p5.js functions setup and draw. If we were to try to use them outside these functions, we would get an error saying that they are not declared.

In this chapter we'll look at another useful variable that p5.js makes available for us: frameCount. We will also learn about frames and frameRate function.

frameCount, frameRate, and frame

Remember how we defined a count function in the previous chapter to be able to count the number of times that the draw function is getting called. We can actually use the variable called frameCount that p5.js provides us for this same purpose. frameCount is a variable that keeps count of the number of times the draw function is called throughout the lifetime of a

© Engin Arslan 2018
E. Arslan, *Learn JavaScript with p5.js*, https://doi.org/10.1007/978-1-4842-3426-6_5

program. By default, the draw function is called a maximum of 60 times per second. A setting called frameRate inside p5.js determines this value.

The introduction of this variable warrants a discussion about what frames are in p5.js. We can think of a frame as the result of the draw function call. The draw function gets called numerous times in a second, and the frameRate function determines this amount. If we are to call the frameRate function with no arguments, it will return us the current frame rate for p5.js - which we can save into a variable and console.log to see its value for every frame (Listing 5-1).

Listing 5-1. Console.log the frame rate

```
function setup() {
        createCanvas(400, 400);
}

function draw() {
        background(220);
        console.log(frameRate());
}
```

The default rate is around 60. This means the draw function will be executed for a maximum amount of 60 times per second. This number depends on our system resources. For performance-related reasons, such as limited system resources, the actual frame rate that can be achieved might be lower than this target value. We can consider 60 as an ideal frame rate that p5.js strives to achieve, but the actual frame rate and hence the performance might be less than this.

Think of frames as sheets in a flip book animation. More sheets viewed per second will mean smoother animation. That's why high frame rates are desirable. The animation might look jaggy if the frame rate is low. We can set the frame rate explicitly in p5.js by passing an integer value to the frameRate function. A frameRate of 1 will have our draw function called every one second.

If we didn't want any animation, then we can call a function called noLoop inside the setup function. This function call will cause the draw function to be called only once.

To summarize, frameCount is the number of times the draw function is executed throughout the lifetime of a program. frameRate is the number of times the draw function is executed in a second. If the frameRate for a program were 60, the frameCount after 3 seconds would be around 60*3=180.

As mentioned earlier, we can see what the current frame rate is by calling the frameRate function with no arguments. But instead of console.log'ing the result, we can actually do much better and display it onscreen.

In p5.js, we can use the text function to display a value to the screen. The text function displays the value that is given as the first argument at the x and y positions that are provided as the second and third arguments (Listing 5-2 and Figure 5-1). With this, we can more easily visualize the frame rate in our program. Please note that the actual result is going to be hard to read at a high frame rate as it fluctuates a lot from one frame to another.

Listing 5-2. Visualize the frame rate

```
function setup() {
        createCanvas(800, 300);
        textAlign(CENTER, CENTER);
}

function draw() {
        background(220);
        fill(237, 34, 93);
        textSize(36);

        // get the current frame rate as an integer.
        var fps = parseInt(frameRate(), 10);
        text("frameRate: " + fps, width/2, height/2);
}
```

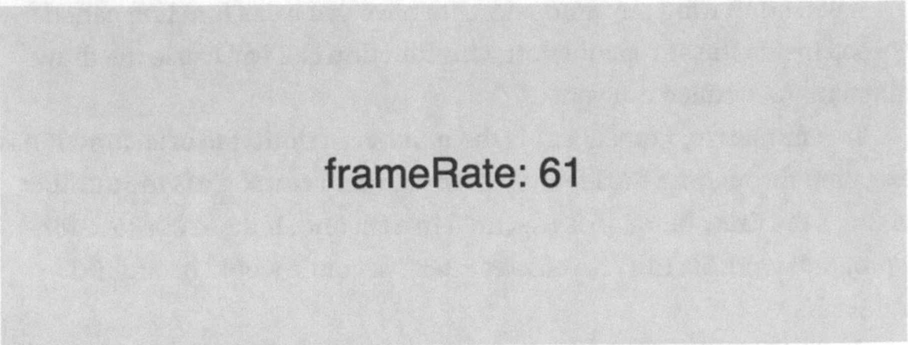

frameRate: 61

Figure 5-1. *Visualize the frame rate*

parseInt is a JavaScript function that allows us to convert a decimal number into an integer. It requires a second argument to signify which number base we are working with (which is almost always going to be 10).

Notice also how in Listing 5-2 we are using a p5.js function called textAlign with the arguments CENTER, CENTER to be able to align the text horizontally and vertically on the screen. Otherwise the text gets drawn from the top-left corner instead of being centered.

We can also try displaying the frameCount variable onscreen (Listing 5-3). As mentioned earlier, this is the variable that holds the number of times the draw function is called.

Listing 5-3. Displaying the frameCount

```
function setup() {
      createCanvas(800, 300);
      textAlign(CENTER, CENTER);
}
```

```
function draw() {
        background(220);
        fill(237, 34, 93);
        textSize(36);

        text("frameCount: " + frameCount, width/2, height/2);
}
```

Using the frameCount variable, we can quickly have a value at our disposal that increments with each execution of the draw function. Notice in Listing 5-4 that the frameCount variable will change more slowly if the frameRate is lower.

Listing 5-4. Using the frameRate variable

```
function setup() {
        createCanvas(800, 300);
        textAlign(CENTER, CENTER);
        frameRate(6); // make animation slower
}

function draw() {
        background(220);
        fill(237, 34, 93);
        textSize(36);

        text("frameCount: " + frameCount, width/2, height/2);
}
```

We could rewrite our example from the earlier chapter to make use of the built-in frameCount variable instead of using our count variable (Listing 5-5).

Listing 5-5. Using the frameCount variable

```
function setup() {
        createCanvas(800, 300);
        rectMode(CENTER);
}

function draw() {
        background(1, 186, 240);

        // declaration of variables
        var x = width / 2;
        var y = height / 2;
        // increment the size with the current frameCount value
        var size = 200 + frameCount;

        // circle
        fill(237, 34, 93);
        noStroke();
        ellipse(x, y, size, size);

        // rectangle
        fill(255);
        rect(x, y, size*0.75, size*0.15);
}
```

Conditionals

So far all the programs we wrote executes in a top-to-bottom, linear fashion. But it is quite common in programming to have some parts of the program to execute only if a certain condition is satisfied. For example, using the variable frameCount, we are now able to animate a shape across the screen, but what if I wanted this animation to start only after a certain frame, like after frame 100?

This can be done using a programming structure called an `if` statement. The `if` statement allows us to execute a block of code only if a certain condition is satisfied. How an `if` statement is written is that we start off with the declaration `if` and inside the parentheses next to it, we write an expression that should evaluate to `true` or `false`. Next, inside curly brackets right after the `if` statement, we write a block of code that we would like to have executed if the expression that we wrote evaluates to `true`:

```
if (<conditional statement>) {
        // do something
}
```

`true` or `false` are actual values in JavaScript just like how numbers are values. They are just a different type of a value than a `Number` or a `String`. They are referred to as `Boolean` values or a `Boolean` data type. Since `true` and `false` are native JavaScript data types, we could type them without any quotation marks and not get an error:

```
console.log(true);
```

We can't get the same result if we are to type `True` or `False` (with the first letter capitalized). Programming languages are particular in how you write things. `True` is not equivalent to `true`. Moreover `True` is not a value that JavaScript recognizes, so writing it without quotation marks will result in an error:

```
console.log(True);
//Uncaught ReferenceError: True is not defined(...)
```

We can also use `comparison` operators to generate `true` or `false` values. Comparison operators allow us to compare two values to each other, and as a result they generate a `true` or `false` value based on the result of that comparison. Here are examples of comparison operators. We have the `bigger-than` symbol `>` that compares two numbers, and if the number on the left-hand side is bigger than the one on the right-hand side it returns `true`; otherwise it returns `false`.

```
console.log(10 > 2); // would evaluate to true
console.log(1 > 100); // false
console.log(100 > 1); //true
```

Bigger or equals >= returns true if the value on the left-hand side is bigger or equal to the value on the right-hand side.

```
console.log(100 >= 100); //true
```

There is also smaller < and smaller or equals <= comparison operators.

```
console.log(1 < 10); //true
console.log(10 <= 10); //true
```

To compare two values to each other to check for equivalency we would use the triple equal sign ===. This is different than what we might be used to from our math classes where the equality operator is a single equal sign operator =. But in JavaScript we already use the single equal sign operator as an assignment operation.

```
console.log(1 === 1); //true
```

We can also make a comparison to check if two values are not equal to each other. For this purpose, we use an exclamation mark in front of the equal sign.

```
console.log(1 !== 1);
```

Make sure to try to use the comparison operations that we learned about to see what kind of results they generate in the console.

Let's look at Listing 5-6 and Figure 5-2 for an example that makes use of if structures.

Listing 5-6. Using the `if` structures

```
var num;

function setup() {
        num = 1;
        createCanvas(800, 300);
        textAlign(CENTER, CENTER);
}

function draw() {
        background(220);
        fill(237, 34, 93);
        textSize(48);

        if (num === 1) {
                // this code gets executed only if num is
                equivalent to 1.
                text('TRUE', width / 2, height / 2);
        }
}
```

Figure 5-2. *Output from Listing 5-6*

The if block will be executed since the expression inside the parentheses will evaluate to true. After all, number one is equivalent to number one. We will see the word TRUE displayed on screen because that's what the code inside the if block does.

If we were to change the value of the num variable to 2, then we won't see anything displayed onscreen because this time, the comparison for the if block will evaluate to false and the conditional will not get executed.

There is this additional structure that can only be used with an if block that is called an else block. An else block follows an if block and gets executed for every other comparison that is not covered by the if block. Let's extend the previous example using an else block (Listing 5-7 and Figure 5-3).

Listing 5-7. Using an else block

```
var num;

function setup() {
        num = 2;
        createCanvas(800, 300);
        textAlign(CENTER, CENTER);
}

function draw() {
        background(220);
        fill(237, 34, 93);
        textSize(48);

        if (num === 1) {
                // this code gets executed only if num is
                equivalent to 1.
                text('TRUE', width / 2, height / 2);
        } else {
```

```
        // this code gets executed if num is NOT
        equivalent to 1.
        text('FALSE', width / 2, height / 2);
    }
}
```

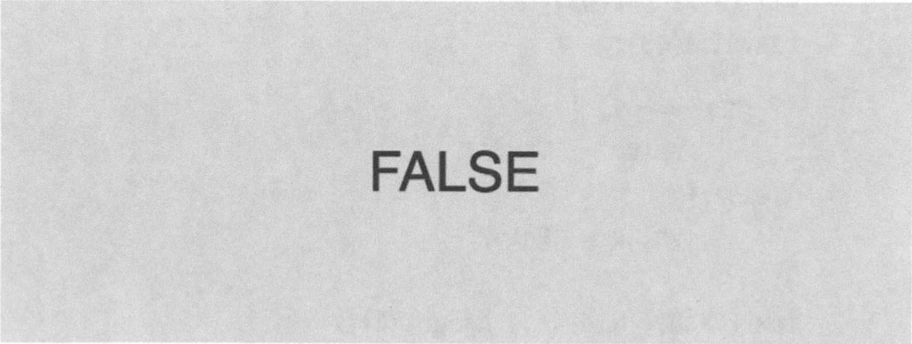

FALSE

Figure 5-3.   *Output from Listing 5-7*

Now in the Listing 5-7 example, the else statement would only get executed whenever the if statement is not executed. That is for every value of the num variable that is not 1.

By the way, notice how we are repeating ourselves by writing the text function twice. We could refactor our code to be a bit more concise (Listing 5-8). Refactoring is, per Wikipedia, the process of restructuring existing computer code — changing the factoring — without changing its external behavior.

Listing 5-8.   Refactoring our code

```
var num;

function setup() {
        num = 2;
        createCanvas(800, 300);
```

```
        textAlign(CENTER, CENTER);
}

function draw() {
        var value;
        background(220);
        fill(237, 34, 93);
        textSize(48);

        if (num === 1) {
                value = 'TRUE';
        } else {
                value = 'FALSE'
        }
        text(value, width/2, height/2);
}
```

The problem with this code before refactoring was that if we wanted
to change the position of the text, we would need to remember to change
it in both text function calls. It might seem easy to remember to do this,
but even small things like this can actually make code maintenance
much harder.

There is one more conditional block that we can add to an if
conditional and that is an else if block. An else if block would allow us
to handle additional conditions. For example, in Listing 5-9 we can add a
couple of else if blocks to the previous example:

Listing 5-9. Using the else if block

```
var num;

function setup() {
        num = 2;
        createCanvas(800, 300);
```

```
        textAlign(CENTER, CENTER);
        fill(237, 34, 93);
}

function draw() {
        var value;
        background(220);
        textSize(48);

        if (num === 1) {
                value = 'TRUE';
        } else if (num === 2) {
                value = 'STILL TRUE';
        } else if (num === 3) {
                value = 'YEP, TRUE';
        } else {
                value = 'FALSE'
        }
        text(value, width/2, height/2);
}
```

Try changing the value of the num variable to see how the code behaves. Using else if blocks, we can handle two more specific conditions for the value of num.

Using what we learned, let's alter the code we wrote in the previous chapter (Listing 4-10) to make the behavior of the animation conditional to the frameCount variable, as shown in Listing 5-10.

Listing 5-10. Making the animation conditional

```
var size;

function setup() {
        createCanvas(800, 300);
        rectMode(CENTER);
```

```
        size = 200;
}

function draw() {
        background(1, 186, 240);

        // declaration of variables
        var x = width / 2;
        var y = height / 2;
        var size = 200;
        if (frameCount < 30) {
                size = size + frameCount;
        } else {
                size = size + 30;
        }

        // ellipse
        fill(237, 34, 93);
        noStroke();
        ellipse(x, y, size, size);

        // rectangle
        fill(255);
        rect(x, y, size*0.75, size*0.15);
}
```

We changed the previous example so that if the frameCount value is less than 30, then the shape will be animated using the frameCount; if not it will remain static.

We can also combine two logical expressions together to create compound statements by using the && or || operators. && stands for AND. This allows us to write expressions that will only evaluate to true only if all parts of the conditional statement is true. Say we wanted to animate the shape only if the frameCount is greater than 20 AND less than 30. We can combine these two conditions using a compound and statement (Listing 5-11).

Listing 5-11. Using a compound and statement

```
if (20 < frameCount && frameCount < 30) {
        size = size + frameCount;
}
```

|| stands for OR. OR compound statements returns true as long as one part of the conditional statement is true. Say we wanted to animate the shape if the frameCount is smaller than 30 OR if the frameCount value is bigger than 120. To express this, we could write the script shown in Listing 5-12.

Listing 5-12. Using a compound or statement

```
if (frameCount < 30 || frameCount > 120) {
        size = size + frameCount;
}
```

Summary

In this chapter, we learned about the concept of frames and how it helps us to create animated images in p5.js.

We also learned about the p5.js frameCount variable that keeps track of how many frames are displayed so far and the frameRate function that allows us to set the frame rate for p5.js.

We learned a couple of other p5.js functions such as the text function that allows us to draw text to the screen and the textAlign function that allows us to align the text that we draw on the screen.

From the JavaScript world, we learned about comparison operators; Boolean data types; `true` and `false`; and most importantly the `if`, `else if`, and `else` conditionals. These structures are commonly used in programming and found in many other programming languages. They allow us to write code that behaves in a little bit more intelligent manner instead of executing blindly from top to bottom.

Practice

Create an animation where five rectangles that are initially offscreen are animated to enter the screen from the left-hand side. They should be moving at different speeds, and they should come to a stop just before exiting the screen.

CHAPTER 6

More p5.js Variables

In the previous chapter, we learned about the p5.js `frameCount` variable that provides us with a number that represents the number of times the `draw` function is called. There are a bunch of other highly useful variables that we could be using in p5.js. We will learn a few more in this chapter.

mouseIsPressed

`mouseIsPressed` is the first p5.js variable that we will see that allows us to add some interactivity to our programs. `mouseIsPressed` is a p5.js variable that assumes the value `true` when the mouse is clicked on the canvas area and `false` for every other time. Let's alter one of the examples from Chapter 4 (Listing 4-10) to quickly see how we can use this variable (Listing 6-1).

Listing 6-1. Conditionally display rectangle inside the circle

```
function setup() {
        createCanvas(800, 300);
        rectMode(CENTER);
}

function draw() {
        background(1, 186, 240);

        // declaration of variables
        var x = width / 2;
```

© Engin Arslan 2018
E. Arslan, *Learn JavaScript with p5.js*, https://doi.org/10.1007/978-1-4842-3426-6_6

```
    var y = height / 2;
    var size = 200; // control the size of the shapes

    // circle
    fill(237, 34, 93);
    noStroke();
    ellipse(x, y, size, size);

    // conditionally display rectangle on mouse press
    if (mouseIsPressed === true) {
        fill(255);
        rect(x, y, size*0.75, size*0.15);
    }
}
```

Clicking on the canvas area will now display the rectangle inside the circle. By using the mouseIsPressed p5.js variable, we made the display of the rectangle conditional to the mouse being pressed.

Toggling the state of something based on a mouse click might be a more involving example, so let's see how to tackle that as well. Say we would like to change the background color for our sketch every time we click the mouse button. In Listing 6-2, we will make it so that it will toggle in between two colors.

Listgin 6-2. Toggle display on mouse click

```
var toggle = true;

function setup() {
        createCanvas(800, 300);
        rectMode(CENTER);
}
```

```
function draw() {
        // change the toggle value based on mouse press.
        if (mouseIsPressed === true) {
                toggle = !toggle;
        }

        // display a different bg color based on the toggle value
        if (toggle === true) {
                background(1, 186, 240);
        } else {
                background(250, 150, 50);
        }

        // declaration of variables
        var x = width / 2;
        var y = height / 2;
        var size = 200;

        // circle
        fill(237, 34, 93);
        noStroke();
        ellipse(x, y, size, size);

        // rectangle
        fill(255);
        rect(x, y, size * 0.75, size * 0.15);
}
```

In this example, we are creating a global variable called toggle that would store a Boolean value. Then we make this Boolean value change to the opposite of what it was with each mouse click by using the exclamation mark operator. When used in front of a Boolean value, the exclamation mark simply inverts the value, meaning it would make a true a false and vice versa.

You might notice that the `mouseIsPressed` variable doesn't seem to work great in capturing our clicks. This is because the `draw` function is being called numerous times in a second, which makes it hard to detect mouse clicks using a conditional. Later, we will see a better way of detecting mouse clicks using p5.js `Events`.

mouseX and mouseY

p5.js variable `mouseX` holds the current horizontal position of the mouse and `mouseY` holds the current vertical position. This sounds simple enough, but they have the potential to enable a great deal of user interaction in our programs and hence are incredibly useful variables. If we are to provide these values as x and y coordinates of a shape, we would essentially be moving that shape as we move our cursor on the screen.

Let's try this with a simplified version of our previous program (Listing 6-1). Listing 6-3 and Figure 6-1 show a version of it with just a circle being drawn in the middle of the screen.

Listing 6-3. Drawing a simple circle to the screen

```
function setup() {
        createCanvas(800, 300);
}

function draw() {
        background(1, 75, 100);

        // declaration of variables
        var x = width / 2;
        var y = height / 2;
        var size = 50;
```

```
    // circle
    fill(237, 34, 93);
    noStroke();
    ellipse(x, y, size, size);
}
```

Figure 6-1. *Drawing a circle*

Now let's use mouseX and mouseY variables for x and y values in Listing 6-4.

Listing 6-4. Using mouseX and mouseY variables

```
function setup() {
    createCanvas(800, 300);
}

function draw() {
    background(1, 75, 100);

    // declaration of variables
    var x = mouseX;
    var y = mouseY;
    var size = 50;
```

```
    // circle
    fill(237, 34, 93);
    noStroke();
    ellipse(x, y, size, size);
}
```

Try moving your mouse on the canvas. Isn't this amazing? By using two built-in variables, we made our otherwise static sketch into something that a user can interact with.

Did you ever wonder why we are setting the background function inside the draw function? We seem to only need to set this value once, so you might have assumed it should go to the setup function.

Placing the background function inside the draw function allows us to override everything that was drawn in the previous frame with a solid color. Without that declaration, at the beginning of the frame, you would notice that drawings from the previous frame persist on the screen. But for certain use cases, this might be exactly what you are going for.

Listing 6-5 and Figure 6-2 show the example from before (Listing 6-4) with a smaller circle size, lower opacity for the shape color, and the background being declared only once in the setup function.

Listing 6-5. Persisting the drawing on the screen

```
function setup() {
    createCanvas(800, 300);
    background(1, 75, 100);
}

function draw() {
    // declaration of variables
    var x = mouseX;
    var y = mouseY;
    var size = 25;
```

```
// circle
fill(237, 34, 93, 100);
noStroke();
ellipse(x, y, size, size);
}
```

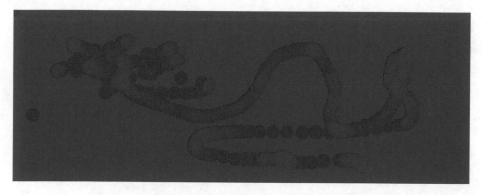

Figure 6-2. *Drawing onscreen using mouseX and mouseY variables*

Summary

In this chapter, we learned about a couple of more p5.js built-in variables that would specifically help us in creating programs that are interactive: programs that can respond to the user action.

We learned about the p5.js `mouseIsPressed` variable that assumes a `true` value whenever the mouse is clicked. But we also learned that this variable might not be the best way to handle user input. We will later see the concept of `Events` in p5.js, which is much better in handling user input.

We also saw `mouseX` and `mouseY` variables and how they can be used to animate objects based on the mouse cursor position, which allows us to add a great deal of interactivity to our programs in an easy manner.

Practice

Build a script that would draw a rectangle to the screen at every mouse click, at the position of the mouse cursor.

CHAPTER 7

Loops

One of things that computers are great at is repetition. Imagine having to create a thousand shapes onscreen with varying parameters. It would take us an unreasonable amount of time to do so with our current programming knowledge. For this kind of case where we want to repeat our code as it is or with variations, we can leverage a programming structure called *loops*. A loop allows us to execute a block of code over and over again.

We are already familiar with the idea of a loop in p5.js. If you think about it, the draw function is a continuous loop that gets executed over and over again until we exit the p5.js program. In this chapter, we will learn how to build this kind of loop ourselves.

For Loop

There are a couple of different kinds of loop structures in JavaScript, but a for loop is by far the most popular. It allows us to repeat an operation for a given amount of times. A for loop has four parts. Listing 7-1 provides an example of how a for loop is constructed.

Listing 7-1. Example of a for loop

```
for (var i = 0; i < 10; i = i + 1) {
        //do something
}
```

© Engin Arslan 2018
E. Arslan, *Learn JavaScript with p5.js*, https://doi.org/10.1007/978-1-4842-3426-6_7

In the first part, we initialize a variable that will keep track of the number of times the loop gets executed – let's call this a counter variable.

```
var i = 0;
```

By convention, inside the for loop, we usually tend to use short variable names like i or j, especially if that variable is only in use for controlling the flow of the for loop. But feel free to use other names as well if it makes sense for your use case.

In the second part, we define a test condition for our loop that gets evaluated each time the loop is about to start. In this example, we are checking to see if our counter variable is smaller than the number 10.

```
i < 10;
```

In the third part, we define a way to update the counter variable that gets evaluated at the end of the loop. In this example, we get the current value of the variable i and add one to it.

```
i = i + 1;
```

Finally, inside curly braces we write the code that we want to have repeated. Once the counter variable doesn't satisfy the test condition, the loop terminates, and the program returns to its normal evaluation.

If the test condition never fails, then we would have a loop that would end up creating an infinite loop, a loop that doesn't have an exit condition so that it keeps going on and on until the program is terminated by external means. The draw function in p5.js is in an infinite loop; it keeps drawing to the screen until we close the browser window.

Even though infinite loops are a valid use case, loops are most commonly used for executing an operation for a known amount of times. Let's create a loop that will draw a given number of ellipses to the screen using a for loop (Listing 7-2 and Figure 7-1).

Listing 7-2. Create ellipses using a `for` loop

```
function setup() {
        createCanvas(800, 300);
}

function draw() {
        background(1, 75, 100);

        // circle properties
        fill(237, 34, 93);
        noStroke();

        for (var i=0; i<10; i=i+1) {
                ellipse(0, 0, 50, 50);
        }
}
```

Figure 7-1. *Output for Listing 7-2*

In our example, we are drawing 10 circles to the screen, but there is no way of visually making that distinction since all the circles are being drawn on top of each other. This is where making use of the loop counter variable can make sense. I can basically use this variable to offset the position of circles each time the loop is called (Listing 7-3 and Figure 7-2).

Listing 7-3. Using a loop counter in a for loop

```
function setup() {
        createCanvas(800, 300);
}

function draw() {
        background(1, 75, 100);

        // circle properties
        fill(237, 34, 93);
        noStroke();

        for (var i=0; i<10; i=i+1) {
                ellipse(i * 50, 0, 50, 50);
        }
}
```

Figure 7-2. *Output for Listing 7-3*

We are multiplying the loop variable by 50 (the diameter of the circle) before feeding into the ellipse function. This allows us to have the shapes not overlap with each other.

Now if we are to execute this, we will see all those circles that the for loop is creating for us. The great thing about this is that since we built the structure for repeating our operations, scaling it up can be as easy as changing the number that we are using inside the loop conditional to a bigger value. Rendering 100 or 1000 circles instead of 10 is just a matter of changing this one value. However, we might start noticing performance degradation if we were to start using huge numbers.

Let's build our code so that we can fill the entire width of the screen with circles (Listing 7-4 and Figure 7-3).

If the width of the screen is 800, and the diameter of a circle is 50 units, then it would mean that we can fill 800 / 50 circles into the width of the page. We would notice a bit of a gap at the end of the page since the first circle is a little bit outside the canvas. We can offset everything to get rid of this gap by adding 25 to the x position, which is half the diameter value. As you already know, we actually don't need to do this math ourselves as we can have JavaScript calculate that value for us.

What you might notice at this point is that we are hard-coding lots of values into our code, and it would be better to use variables instead for flexibility. We will refactor our code to do so.

Listing 7-4. Filling the screen width with circles

```
function setup() {
        createCanvas(800, 300);
}

function draw() {
        background(1, 75, 100);

        // circle properties
        fill(237, 34, 93);
        noStroke();
        var diameter = 50;
```

```
for (var i=0; i< width/diameter; i=i+1) {
        ellipse(diameter/2 + i * diameter, 0, diameter,
        diameter);
    }
}
```

Figure 7-3. *Output for Listing 7-4*

Now, if we are to change a single value, the diameter of the circle, the entire code will still draw just enough circles to fill the screen. That's a pretty impressive thing to have.

What if we wanted to fill the height of the screen with circles as well? To be able to do this, we need to write another for loop that would place circles for the entire length of the canvas for each circle that is placed for the width. This requires us to place a second loop inside the first one, effectively *nesting* a loop inside another loop. See Listing 7-5 and Figure 7-4.

Listing 7-5. Filling the screen with circles

```
function setup() {
    createCanvas(800, 300);
}
```

```
function draw() {
        background(1, 75, 100);

        // circle properties
        fill(237, 34, 93);
        noStroke();
        var diameter = 50;

        for (var i=0; i<width/diameter; i=i+1) {
                for (var j=0; j<height/diameter; j=j+1) {
                        ellipse(
                                diameter/2 + i * diameter,
                                diameter/2 + j * diameter,
                                diameter,
                                diameter
                        );
                }
        }
}
```

Figure 7-4. *Output for Listing 7-5*

Notice the way we declared the `ellipse` function in this example. We are writing it over multiple lines to be able to increase the legibility. JavaScript doesn't care about the whitespace so writing our code using multiple lines doesn't result in any errors.

This code is pretty useful right now. For one thing, it is robust; we could be changing the size of the drawing area or the number of circles being drawn, but things will still continue to function properly.

Something to keep in mind is this: putting loops inside one another can make our program really slow due to the number of operations that need to be performed. Also, sometimes nested structures can make our programs hard to read as well.

Random and Noise Functions

Since we can now create loops that make use of a different value each time they are executed, it might be a good time to learn about the p5.js `random` function. The p5.js `random` function generates a random number every time it's called. This is useful when we want to use random values for the parameters of the shapes we are drawing.

If we call the `random` function without any parameters, then it would result in a random number between 0 and 1 for each `draw` function call or each frame. If we provide a value to the `random` function, then it would return a random value that is above 0 and below the given value. If we provide two values to the `random` function, then we would get a random value that is in between the given two numbers. See Listing 7-6 for examples of these situations.

Listing 7-6. Examples of using the `random` function

```
console.log(random()); // a random number in between 0 and 1
console.log(random(10)); // a random number in between 0 and 10
console.log(random(100, 1000)); // a random number in between
100 and 1000
```

Listing 7-7 is a small script for using the random function in different ways. Figure 7-5 shows the results of that script. Numbers that are displayed are randomly generated and will be different each time the code is executed.

Listing 7-7. Using the random function

```
function setup() {
        createCanvas(800, 300);
        textAlign(CENTER, CENTER);
        fill(237, 34, 93);
        frameRate(1);
}

function draw() {
        var random_0 = random();
        var random_1 = random(10);
        var random_2 = random(100, 1000);
        var offset = 40;

        textSize(24);
        background(255);
        text(random_0, width/2, height/2-offset);
        text(random_1, width/2, height/2-0);
        text(random_2, width/2, height/2+offset);
}
```

0.9508755624735825

3.0819398604499737

435.0809715882096

Figure 7-5. *Output from Listing 7-7*

With Listing 7-8 and Figure 7-6, let's update our previous code (Listing 7-5) to make use of the random function.

Listing 7-8. Using the random function

```
function setup() {
      createCanvas(800, 300);
}

function draw() {
      background(1, 75, 100);

      // circle properties
      fill(237, 34, 93);
      noStroke();
      var diameter = 50;

      for (var i=0; i<width/diameter; i=i+1) {
            for (var j=0; j<height/diameter; j=j+1) {
                  ellipse(
                        diameter/2 + i * diameter,
                        diameter/2 + j * diameter,
```

```
                         diameter * random(), // using
                         the random function
                         diameter
              );
          }
      }
}
```

Figure 7-6. *Output from Listing 7-8*

We are using the result of the random function to multiply the width of the ellipse with a random number that would be a value in between 0 and 1 each time the random function is called. Since the random function can assume any value in its range in any frame, the animation looks pretty aggressive. If we want randomness that changes gradually, and hence looks a bit more organic, then we should look into the noise function.

We can feed any numeric value to the noise function and it would return a semi-random value in between 0 and 1. It would always return the same output for the given value. The good thing about the noise function is that if the value we feed to the noise function changes only incrementally, then the output value will only change incrementally as well. This will result in a smooth transition between the random values we are getting back.

To be able to conceptualize how the noise function works, we can think of an infinite amount of random values that are changing gradually like a wave, and the values that we provide to the noise function are like coordinates for these random values. Essentially we are just sampling an already existing noise. Whenever we provide the noise function with the same values, we are going to receive the same semi-random value in return.

We will rewrite the above program (Listing 7-8) to make use of noise function instead. We will feed the noise function with the frameCount variable since it is a good way of getting sequential numbers in p5.js. But we will divide the frameCount with 100 to be able to slow down the change of values and hence the resulting animation a bit. See Listing 7-9 and Figure 7-7.

Listing 7-9. Using the noise function

```
function setup() {
        createCanvas(800, 300);
}

function draw() {
        background(1, 75, 100);

        // circle properties
        fill(237, 34, 93);
        noStroke();
        var diameter = 50;

        for (var i=0; i<width/diameter; i=i+1) {
                for (var j=0; j<height/diameter; j=j+1) {
                        ellipse(
                                diameter/2 + i * diameter,
                                diameter/2 + j * diameter,
```

```
                         diameter * noise(frameCount/100),
                         // using then noise function
                         diameter * noise(frameCount/100)
                         // using then noise function
              );
        }
    }
}
```

Figure 7-7. Output from Listing 7-9

Notice how all the shapes are using the same animation right now. What if we wanted to get a different noise value for each one of these shapes? Currently we have the values repeating since the noise function, when provided with the same values, returns the same output. To be able to get a different output value for each of the shapes, we might want to rewrite the above function to make use of i and j values of the for loop to adjust where the noise is being sampled from. See Listing 7-10 and Figure 7-8.

Listing 7-10. Applying a different animation to each circle

```
function setup() {
        createCanvas(800, 300);
}

function draw() {
        background(1, 75, 100);

        // circle properties
        fill(237, 34, 93);
        noStroke();
        var diameter = 50;

        for (var i=0; i<width/diameter; i=i+1) {
                for (var j=0; j<height/diameter; j=j+1) {
                        ellipse(
                                diameter/2 + i * diameter,
                                diameter/2 + j * diameter,
                                // applying a different
                                animation to each circle
                                diameter * noise(frameCount/100 +
                                j*10000 + i*10000),
                                // applying a different
                                animation to each circle
                                diameter * noise(frameCount/100 +
                                j*10000 + i*10000)
                        );
                }
        }
}
```

Figure 7-8. *Output from Listing 7-10*

The value 10000 we are using above as a multiplier is completely arbitrary. We are just trying to make sure that the coordinates we provide to the noise function are farther apart from each other.

Summary

Loops are one of the most powerful structures in programming. They allow us to tap into the true computational power of computers, repeating operations on a larger scale that could be impossible for a human to perform in a reasonable amount of time.

In this chapter we learned about how to build for loops and how to nest loops in each other to get a grid of repeating shapes instead of just a line of them.

We also learned about the p5.js random and noise functions and the differences between them.

Practice

Create a loop that would create an array of rectangles that have their color changed gradually from black to white (Figure 7-9). You should build the loop in such a way that a single variable would control the number of rectangles drawn.

Figure 7-9. *Practice image*

CHAPTER 8

Functions

Functions are primary building blocks of JavaScript. They allow us to write programs in a more efficient and scalable manner. Functions help us to manage complexity by containing and grouping operations under a single executable name. We already know how to call functions by using the p5.js predefined functions such as `ellipse` or `background`. We even declared our own functions as p5.js forces us to put our code into two function declarations: `setup` and `draw`. If we wanted to create our own functions, we would follow the same convention we have been using for the creation, or declaration, of these functions.

Creating Functions

To create (or declare) a new function, we would start off by using the `function` keyword and then give the function a name of our choosing that ideally describes the behavior or purpose of the function. See Listing 8-1.

Listing 8-1. Creating a function

```
function functionName() {
        // function body
}
```

Next to the function name we would open brackets. If we want to build a function that works with user input, we can define parameters inside the brackets that act as placeholder variable names for the future user input. We will see how this works in a bit.

© Engin Arslan 2018
E. Arslan, *Learn JavaScript with p5.js*, https://doi.org/10.1007/978-1-4842-3426-6_8

Then we have curly braces. Inside the curly braces can be referred to as the function body. In there, we write the code that constructs the logic of the function. We can also make use of the parameters, the variable names we defined inside the brackets next to the function name, as part of the operations we want to perform inside the function body.

Let's look at a simple example. Notice how p5.js has an `ellipse` function but not a `circle` function. This is not really an issue since we can easily create a circle by providing the `ellipse` function with the same width and height values. For argument's sake, though, let's create a `circle` function that would work with three values: the x and y position that we want to draw our circle at and the diameter of the circle.

Listing 8-2 shows how to do it. Inside the brackets, we will write down variable names that will eventually be provided when this function is called. These names are called *parameters* as they parameterize the functionality of the operation we are creating. We will use these parameters inside our function to allow the user to control the inner workings of the function.

Listing 8-2. Declaring a circle function

```
function circle(x, y, diameter) {
        ellipse(x, y, diameter, diameter);
}
```

We can choose anything as parameter names, but it usually makes sense to use names that communicate the intent clearly. So in our case, using the names x, y, and `diameter` make sense.

After defining this function, we can call it by using its name and providing it with values. Values provided to the function are called *arguments* to the function. Notice that the function might fail or not work as expected if all the required arguments are not provided (Listing 8-3).

Listing 8-3. Calling the circle function

```
circle(width/2, height/2, 100);
```

Don't worry too much if you feel like the terminology is confusing. It might take some time to get used to it. The *parameters* of a function can be thought as the values that the user would eventually provide when they are using the function. Those same values that are provided when calling the function are referred to as *arguments*.

With the `circle` function, we don't need to worry about using the `ellipse` function to draw circles anymore. We can just use our own function to draw those perfectly round circles. Having implemented the `circle` function ourselves, we know that it actually uses the `ellipse` function under the hood to draw those circles. But the neat thing about functions is that we don't really need to know how they work once they are available to us. We can just use them without thinking how they are implemented. The `ellipse` function that is implemented by the smart people who created p5.js might be using all sorts of things inside to draw an ellipse, but as far as we are concerned, it draws an ellipse when it is called, and that's all that matters.

In this example, creating a `circle` function doesn't buy us too much efficiency. As a matter of fact, we can just pass three arguments to the `ellipse` function instead of four to draw a circle instead. But functions become really important to use when we are building more complex programs. They help us manage the complexity by containing and grouping operations under a single executable name. Functions are essentially black boxes. They encapsulate the code contained inside. Additionally, whatever variables are declared using the `var` keyword inside the function are not visible from outside the function. This means that calling them from outside of the function that they are defined in will result in an error. See Listing 8-4 for an example.

Listing 8-4. Variable visibility (scope)

```
function setup() {
        createCanvas(800, 300);
        sayHello();
}

function draw() {
        background(220);
}

function sayHello() {
        var message = 'Hello World!';
        console.log(message);
}

console.log(message); // this line will throw an error
```

The `console.log` function on line 15 will throw an error because the variable `message` is only visible from inside the function `sayHello`.

Functions can work with no input, a single input, or multiple inputs; and they either return a result or they don't. Let me explain what I mean by returning a value.

Let's say we want to create a function that multiplies a given numeric value by itself, essentially calculating the square of the given number. Listing 8-5 shows one function that does that. It receives a number as a parameter and creates text that displays that number on the screen. So it is somewhat useful since we can use this function to display the square of a number on the screen. Results are shown in Figure 8-1.

Listing 8-5. Creating a multiplying function

```
function setup() {
        createCanvas(800, 300);
}
```

```
function draw() {
        background(1, 75, 100);
        squared(10);
}

function squared(num) {
        fill(237, 34, 93);
        textSize(60);
        textAlign(CENTER, CENTER);
        text(num * num, width/2, height/2);
}
```

Figure 8-1. *Output from Listing 8-5*

But if we wanted to use this resulting number in another calculation, we might hit a roadblock. This function is not *returning* the number to us; it is just displaying it on the screen. Calling this function affects the environment that we are in, but it doesn't *return* a value for it to be used in further calculations. Some of the functions we have seen so far, like ellipse, rect, etc..., behaved in a similar fashion where they do something but don't actually return a value as a result of that calculation. However, the random function when executed doesn't display anything on the screen but returns a value that we can capture in a variable.

To be able to return values from a function, we can use the return keyword. Let's alter the squared function to both: display the results on the screen and also to return a value (Listing 8-6).

Listing 8-6. Using the return keyword

```
function setup() {
        createCanvas(800, 300);
}

function draw() {
        background(1, 75, 100);
        var x = squared(10);
        console.log(x);
}

function squared(num) {
        fill(237, 34, 93);
        textSize(60);
        textAlign(CENTER, CENTER);
        var result = num * num;
        text(result, width/2, height/2);

        // return the value of the result from the function
        return result;
}
```

Now, this function returns a value that we are using in a console.log function. Whenever the program comes across the keyword return, the program terminates the execution of the function and returns the value that is declared next to it – to the caller of the function. This means that if we had any other lines below the return keyword, they wouldn't get executed since return terminates the execution of the current function.

The `return` keyword is only available inside functions. Trying to use it from outside a function will result in an error. As outside of a function, there is nothing to be returned.

Revisiting Setup and Draw Functions

Now that we learned about creating our functions, it is important to emphasize the difference between declaring a function versus calling a function. Notice how when we created our functions that we had to call them in order for them to be executed. For example, in this code example in Listing 8-7, we are only creating or declaring a function:

Listing 8-7. Creating and declaring a function

```
function myFunction() {
}
```

To be able to make use of this function, we need to execute it, by calling it with its name and using parentheses next to that name, as shown in Listing 8-8.

Listing 8-8. Calling a function

```
myFunction();
```

Notice one thing slightly strange when working in p5.js. We never really call the `setup` and `draw` functions and yet they get executed anyway! This is due to how p5.js is architected. p5.js handles the execution of the `setup` and `draw` functions for us as their execution follows some simple rules that are the following:

- `setup` function gets executed before the `draw` function.

- `setup` function is only executed one time, whereas `draw` function is executed continuously at a certain default rate.

107

Summary

We have made use of functions from the moment we started to use p5.js. Its very own architecture depends on the existence of two functions inside our programs that has to have the name `setup` and `draw`. Moreover, we have been using functions that come with the p5.js library such as `ellipse`, `rect`, etc.

We have seen that functions can be built to work with external user input or not. We can also build functions that either return a value using the `return` keyword or not.

Functions are a way to create modular blocks of code that can be reused throughout our code. These functions make our programs more maintainable and scalable by decreasing the amount of code we need to write. Whenever we find ourselves repeating a block of code in multiple places, it's likely a good candidate to create a function from.

Practice

Create a function called `grid` that would work with three parameters: a `numX` and a `numY` parameter that would create `numX` amount of shapes (say rectangles) on the x-axis and `numY` amount of shapes on the y-axis and a `size` parameter that would set the size of the shapes.

For example:

```
grid(10, 30, 20); // Would create 10 x 30 rectangles of size
20px.
```

CHAPTER 9

Objects

JavaScript contains a data structure called Objects. Objects help you organize code and they make it easier to work with in certain cases. There are two ways of creating objects: by using an object initializer or by using constructor functions. In this chapter we'll create a single object using an object initializer, while constructor functions act as a blueprint from which we can create many object instances using the new keyword.

Using Object Initializer

JavaScript uses a data structure called Object that helps organize data together. There are a couple of ways of creating an object in JavaScript. One way is by using the curly brackets, as seen in Listing 9-1.

Listing 9-1. Creating an object with curly brackets

```
var colors = {};
```

These curly brackets are called Object Initializer. They create an empty object. We hold a reference to the object by using the variable colors.

Now we can add properties to this colors object by providing the desired property names after a dot. This is called *dot notation*. We will also assign values to these newly created properties. See Listing 9-2.

© Engin Arslan 2018
E. Arslan, *Learn JavaScript with p5.js*, https://doi.org/10.1007/978-1-4842-3426-6_9

Listing 9-2. Adding properties to an object

```
var colors = {};
colors.black = 0;
colors.darkGray = 55;
colors.gray = 125;
colors.lightGray = 175;
colors.white = 255;

console.log(colors);
```

If we are to look at the object at this point by using `console.log`, we would see it looks something like this:

```
{"black":0,"darkGray":55,"gray":125,"lightGray":175,
"white":255}
```

We could also have created an object with the same properties from the get go, by providing these properties inside the curly brackets (Listing 9-3).

Listing 9-3. Adding properties inside the curly brackets

```
var colors = {
        black: 0,
        darkGray: 55,
        gray: 125,
        lightGray: 175,
        white: 255,
};

console.log(colors);
```

Objects are basically *key-value* pairs. Each key stores a *value* and each *key-value* pair makes up a *property* on an object.

As shown in Listing 9-4, to access a value on an object, we can again use the dot notation.

110

Listing 9-4. Access a value of an object

```
console.log(colors.gray);
```

For some situations, the dot notation doesn't work. An example of this is when we use numbers as our key values in an object. In that case, we can use square brackets to access values instead. See Listing 9-5.

Listing 9-5. Use square brackets to access values

```
console.log(colors[1]); // Assuming you were using numbers
                        instead of color names as key values.
```

What do you think this above expression will return if we were to console.log it? We would get the value undefined as the key 1 doesn't exist in our current colors object.

We can also define functions as values for keys in an object. In that case, the resulting property would be referred to as a *method*.

Continuing from our colors object, let's define a method inside that object called paintItBlack, which would make the background color be black (Listing 9-6).

Listing 9-6. Defining a method

```
var colors = {
        black: 0,
        darkGray: 55,
        gray: 125,
        lightGray: 175,
        white: 255,
        paintItBlack: function() {
                background(this.black);
        }
};
```

Listing 9-7 shows a p5.js code that makes use of this object.

Listing 9-7. Using an object

```
var colors;

function setup() {
        createCanvas(800, 300);

        colors = {
                black: 0,
                darkGray: 55,
                gray: 125,
                lightGray: 175,
                white: 255,
                paintItBlack: function() {
                        background(this.black);
                }
        };
}

function draw() {
        background(220);

        // calling the paintItBlack method after frame 120.
        if (frameCount > 120) {
                colors.paintItBlack();
        }
}
```

In this example, we are initializing the `colors` variable outside the scope of the `setup` and `draw` functions and then creating its content inside the `setup` function. After all, we only need the content to be created once. And then we call its `paintItBlack` method if the `frameCount` is bigger than 120, which would happen after two seconds with default settings.

(Remember the default value for the frameRate is 60, which means that approximately 60 frames are rendered per second.)

To be able to use a key that is defined inside the object from within, we need to be able to refer to the object itself. In JavaScript, there is a keyword called this, which allows us to do so (Listing 9-8). Using the this keyword, we can refer to the keys that are defined on the object itself.

Listing 9-8. Using the this keyword

```
paintItBlack: function() {
        background(this.black);
}
```

Once we have defined a method on the object, we can call the method by accessing it using the dot notation (Listing 9-9). Since we are executing a function in this instance, we need to have brackets after the function name.

Listing 9-9. Calling the method

```
colors.paintItBlack();
```

The concept of objects in JavaScript (or in other languages that implement objects) exists so that we can model after real-world objects or concepts. Just like how real-world objects have properties and sometimes a behavior, programming language objects can have properties that describe what they are and methods that specify how they behave.

With Listing 9-10, let me give you an example of a programming language object that models after a real-world concept. We will create an object called circle. This circle object will have several properties defining how it looks, and also it will have several methods that describe how it behaves.

Listing 9-10. Creating an object

```
var circle = {
        x: width/2,
        y: height/2,
        size: 50,
};
```

This `circle` object has an x and y property that defines its coordinates and a `size` property that defines its size. We will also create a method on it, a property that is a function, which defines a certain behavior (Listing 9-11). In this case, the defined behavior will be to draw the circle to the screen.

Listing 9-11. Adding a draw method to the circle object

```
var circle = {
        x: width/2,
        y: height/2,
        size: 50,
        draw: function() {
                ellipse(this.x, this.y, this.size, this.size);
        },
};
```

In this example, we are again using the `this` keyword to be able to access the properties on an object. The `this` keyword basically refers to the object itself and allows us to call the object's properties while inside the object. We can now draw this circle on the screen by using the `circle.draw()` method call:

```
circle.draw();
```

You must be thinking to yourself: this was the most convoluted thing ever. Because why should we ever need to draw a circle this way when we can just call a function to draw it onscreen (Listing 9-12)?

Listing 9-12. Using the ellipse function to draw a circle to the screen

```
ellipse(width/2, height/2, 50, 50);
```

We are just getting started, though. Let's add another method to the circle called grow, which would increase the size of the circle by one unit whenever it's called (Listing 9-13).

Listing 9-13. Adding grow method

```
var circle = {
        x: width/2,
        y: height/2,
        size: 50,
        draw: function() {
                ellipse(this.x, this.y, this.size, this.size);
        },
        grow: function() {
                if (this.size < 200) {
                        this.size += 1;
                }
        },
};
```

Now, if we are to call this function inside the draw function, we would see our circle keep growing as the draw function is continuously called by p5.js. Listing 9-14 provides the whole example. Figure 9-1 shows the resulting output.

Listing 9-14. Using the circle object

```
var circle;

function setup() {
        createCanvas(800, 300);

        circle = {
                x: width/2,
                y: height/2,
                size: 50,
                draw: function() {
                        ellipse(this.x, this.y, this.size,
                        this.size);
                },
                grow: function() {
                        if (this.size < 200) {
                                this.size += 1;
                        }
                },
        };
}

function draw() {
        background(220);

        // circle properties
        fill(237, 34, 93);
        noStroke();

        circle.draw();
        circle.grow();
}
```

Figure 9-1. *Output from Listing 9-14*

As mentioned earlier, the usage of objects is about code organization. We don't have separate functions that manipulate the circle, but we have a `circle` object that carries those functions and its properties within itself. This can make our code easier to reason about in certain cases.

Using the Constructor Function

There is another way to create objects in JavaScript, and that is by using functions (Listing 9-15). The declarations we make inside an object that is creating a function is very similar to what we were doing when working with an *object initializer*. Notice how we are using the `width` and `height` p5.js variables inside the function. For these variables to be available to this function, it needs to be called after the `createCanvas` function.

Listing 9-15. Using a function to create an object

```
var Circle = function() {
        this.x = width/2;
        this.y = height/2;
        this.size = 50;
```

```
       this.draw = function() {
               ellipse(this.x, this.y, this.size, this.size);
       };
       this.grow = function() {
               if (this.size < 200) {
                       this.size += 1;
               }
       };
};
```

An object-creating function is called a `constructor` `function`. We can think of it as a template or a blueprint for creating new objects that derive their properties from this constructor function.

Listing 9-16 shows an example to better explain what I mean. Say we want to have a circle just like in the previous examples that exhibits the behavior that is defined by this `Circle` constructor. In this case, we will not use this constructor function directly for our purposes, but we will use it to instantiate a new circle that is modeled after this template function.

Listing 9-16. Using a constructor function

```
var myCircle = new Circle();
```

We used the `Circle` constructor function and the new keyword to create a new instance of a circle called `myCircle` that gets its properties from the constructor function. Basically, the new keyword allows us to create a new instance of an object from a constructor function. We can think of the `Circle` constructor function as a blueprint and the `myCircle` as an actual circle built from that blueprint. Now we can draw this newly created circle to the screen by calling the `draw` method on it (Listing 9-17).

Listing 9-17. Calling the draw method

```
myCircle.draw();
```

Listing 9-18 provides the full example.

Listing 9-18. Using a constructor function

```
var circle;

function setup() {
        createCanvas(800, 300);

        // instantiating a new circle using the Circle
        Constructor Function
        circle = new Circle();
}

function draw() {
        background(220);

        // circle properties
        fill(237, 34, 93);
        noStroke();

        circle.draw();
        circle.grow();
}

var Circle = function() {
        this.x = width/2;
        this.y = height/2;
        this.size = 50;
        this.draw = function() {
                ellipse(this.x, this.y, this.size, this.size);
        };
```

```
        this.grow = function() {
                if (this.size < 200) {
                        this.size += 1;
                }
        };
};
```

The beauty of this method is that we can keep creating new circles from the same blueprint. And since these circles are separate entities or instances, they can have different properties from each other. Let's see an example of that in Listing 9-19 and Figure 9-2.

Listing 9-19. Creating separate circle instances

```
var circle_1;
var circle_2;
var circle_3;

function setup() {
        createCanvas(800, 300);

        // instantiating circles
        circle_1 = new Circle();
        circle_2 = new Circle();
        circle_3 = new Circle();
}

function draw() {
        background(220);

        // circle properties
        fill(237, 34, 93);
        noStroke();
```

```
        circle_1.draw();
        circle_1.grow();

        circle_2.x = 150;
        circle_2.draw();
        circle_2.grow();

        circle_3.x = 650;
        circle_3.draw();
        circle_3.grow();
}

var Circle = function() {
        this.x = width / 2;
        this.y = height / 2;
        this.size = 50;
        this.draw = function() {
                ellipse(this.x, this.y, this.size, this.size);
        };
        this.grow = function() {
                if (this.size < 200) {
                        this.size += 1;
                }
        };
};
```

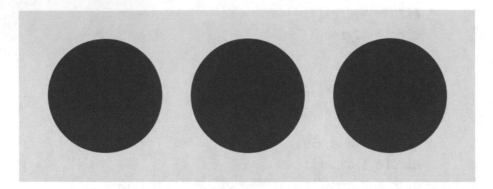

Figure 9-2. *Output from Listing 9-19*

In this example, we are creating three variables outside the p5.js functions called `circle_1`, `circle_2`, and `circle_3`. These variables are created outside the p5.js functions so that they would be in scope for both of those functions.

We are making these variables to be `Circle` instances by assigning the `Circle` constructor function using the `new` keyword to them. Now that we have three separate circle objects, we can change their properties in the `draw` function, and we get different results from each one of them.

One thing that is important to note is how we are using a function name that starts with a capital letter for the constructor function. We use a capital letter to remind ourselves and others that this function is a constructor function and needs to be called with the `new` keyword.

It is important to call a constructor function with the `new` keyword. If we don't, it won't work properly, as the `this` keyword inside the constructor function wouldn't refer to the instance object but the global object.

Usage of the capital letter is not a rule but a convention. No one forces us to do it. But it is expected that we follow this convention since not realizing a function is a constructor function, and then calling it without the `new` keyword will have unintended consequences.

Summary

In this chapter, we learned about the JavaScript objects. Simply put, objects are a way of organizing code. There are two ways of creating objects. One of the ways is using an `object initializer`, and the other one is using `constructor functions`.

We also learned about the dot notation and the square bracket notation that are used to access the properties on an object. The `this` keyword allows us to refer to the properties of the object from within the object itself.

There is a whole programming paradigm called *Object-Oriented Programming* across different programming languages that leverages the usage of objects for code organization and clarity. Using p5.js, we don't necessarily need to create objects to organize our code, but I wanted to introduce objects for two reasons:

- They are a fundamental part of the JavaScript Language. If you would like to learn more about the language at a later time, you would need to get comfortable with how objects work.

- JavaScript has other built-in structures that are based on objects we will be using, so it was important for us to further familiarize ourselves with objects.

CHAPTER 10

Arrays

Arrays are another useful data structure in JavaScript. They are a sequential collection of data stored with a numbered index and are based on Objects, which make certain operations much easier to perform.

In this chapter we'll populate an array using the push method. We'll also learn about the remainder operator, which we can use to derive sequential values that cycle in between zero and the desired value.

Using the push Method

Remember that we use curly brackets to create an empty object. We can create an empty array in a similar fashion by using square brackets (Listing 10-1).

Listing 10-1. Create an empty array

```
var arr = [];
```

In this example, we created an empty array and used a variable called arr to store that array. Now if we wanted to add elements to this array, we can use the push method that array objects have (Listing 10-2).

© Engin Arslan 2018
E. Arslan, *Learn JavaScript with p5.js*, https://doi.org/10.1007/978-1-4842-3426-6_10

Listing 10-2. Adding elements to the array

```
var arr = [];
arr.push(1);
arr.push("hello world");
arr.push({"name":"value"});
console.log(arr);
```

In this example, we are pushing three new values to the previously empty array. In the first line, we are pushing in a value of number type, in the second line we are pushing a string type into the array, and in the third line we are pushing an object type into it.

Now if we are to look at the contents of the array by using console.log, we will see something like this onscreen:

```
[1,"hello world",{"name":"value"}]
```

Notice how we used different data types and objects to populate the Array. Arrays can contain any object, even other arrays. Just like how it is with JavaScript objects, we can populate an Array at creation time by providing desired values inside square brackets using a comma to separate them. Let's create an array with four numbers in it (Listing 10-3).

Listing 10-3. Creating an array with different data types

```
var arr = [15, 40, 243, 53];
console.log(arr);
```

We can use the index number property that is automatically generated to access the individual items in an array. One thing to know, though, is the indices that refer to the stored items in an array start counting from 0. To access an individual item in an array, we can type the variable name that the array is stored in, and then use the index number in square brackets to refer to that item at that index (see Listing 10-4). The number 0 will refer to the first item in the array - which is 15 -, the index number 1 will be for the second item, etc...

Listing 10-4. Accessing the items of an array

```
var arr = [15, 40, 243, 53];
var firstItem = arr[0];
console.log(firstItem);
```

If we try to access an item that doesn't exist, we will get an undefined value. This makes sense because that item is not defined. Remember objects also return an undefined value when we try to access a property that doesn't exist.

Let's see how the array data structure can simplify things when building programs. We will start with a simple example (Listing 10-5). Imagine we want to create five different circles of distinct sizes. To be able to do so with our current knowledge, we would need to create five different variables and assign those variables the desired values. And then we call the ellipse function five times, using a different variable each time.

Listing 10-5. Drawing circles of different sizes

```
var size1 = 200;
var size2 = 150;
var size3 = 100;
var size4 = 50;
var size5 = 25;

function setup() {
        createCanvas(800, 300);
}
```

```
function draw() {
        // circle properties
        fill(237, 34, 93);
        strokeWeight(2);

        ellipse(width/2, height/2, size1, size1);
        ellipse(width/2, height/2, size2, size2);
        ellipse(width/2, height/2, size3, size3);
        ellipse(width/2, height/2, size4, size4);
        ellipse(width/2, height/2, size5, size5);
}
```

We are only drawing five circles to the screen, but this is already looking like a burdensome solution. What if we needed to draw 100 circles or even 1000? This is where arrays come into play and make our job much easier.

First, let's create an array of desired circle sizes. As mentioned earlier, we can use the index numbers to access the individual items in an array. We will use this knowledge to fetch the desired values from our array. See Listing 10-6.

Listing 10-6. Using an array to store the size values

```
var sizes = [200, 150, 100, 50, 25];

function setup() {
        createCanvas(800, 300);
}

function draw() {
        // circle properties
        fill(237, 34, 93);
        strokeWeight(2);
```

```
    ellipse(width/2, height/2, sizes[0], sizes[0]);
    ellipse(width/2, height/2, sizes[1], sizes[1]);
    ellipse(width/2, height/2, sizes[2], sizes[2]);
    ellipse(width/2, height/2, sizes[3], sizes[3]);
    ellipse(width/2, height/2, sizes[4], sizes[4]);
}
```

This is already looking so much better. But notice the amount of repetition that's still happening. We are essentially typing the same thing over and over again when calling the ellipse function; the only thing that's changing is the index numbers. A very clear pattern is emerging here: if we had a structure that would create a loop for us to call ellipse function five times with increasing values, then we won't have to repeat ourselves.

Luckily, we know how to create a *for loop* that will help us to do precisely that. Listing 10-7 provides the above code rewritten to use a *for loop*.

Listing 10-7. A for-loop snippet

```
var sizes = [200, 150, 100, 50, 25];
for (var i = 0; i < 5; i++) {
        ellipse(width / 2, height / 2, sizes[i], sizes[i]);
}
```

Listing 10-8 and Figure 10-1 shows the usage of the code inside a p5.js example:

Listing 10-8. Entire code using for loop

```
var sizes = [200, 150, 100, 50, 25];

function setup() {
        createCanvas(800, 300);
}
```

```
function draw() {
        // circle properties
        fill(237, 34, 93);
        strokeWeight(2);

        for (var i = 0; i < 5; i++) {
                ellipse(width / 2, height / 2, sizes[i],
                sizes[i]);
        }
}
```

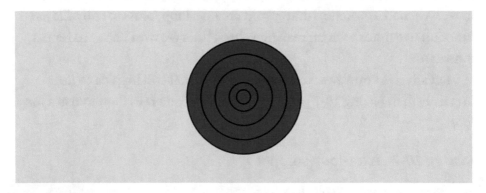

Figure 10-1. *Circles drawn using a for loop*

Notice the usage of the number five inside the for loop header? It is there because the array we are using has five items in it. So if there were six items, then we should update this value to six. But this is a bit problematic; what if we made our array bigger but forgot to update this value? Luckily we can use an array property called length instead, which would give us the number of items in an array. We can rewrite the above code to make use of the length property (Listing 10-9).

Listing 10-9. Using the array height property

```
var sizes = [200, 150, 100, 50, 25];

function setup() {
        createCanvas(800, 300);
}

function draw() {
        // circle properties
        fill(237, 34, 93);
        strokeWeight(2);

        for (var i = 0; i < sizes.length; i++) {
                ellipse(width / 2, height / 2, sizes[i],
                sizes[i]);
        }
}
```

Our code is much more concise now, and it is insanely scalable as well. We can just keep adding new values to the sizes array, and an equal amount of circles will be drawn for us. Just for fun, let's automate this setup even further. Currently, we are manually creating the array that has the size values. But we could create another for loop that would populate this array with any amount of random numbers of our choosing by using the random function (see Listing 10-10 and Figure 10-2).

Listing 10-10. Using the random function

```
var sizes = [];

function setup() {
        createCanvas(800, 600);
        noFill();
```

```
        // populating the sizes array with random values
        for (var i=0; i<100; i++) {
                var randomValue = random(5, 500);
                sizes.push(randomValue);
        }
}

function draw() {
        background(255);
        for (var i = 0; i < sizes.length; i++) {
                ellipse(width / 2, height / 2, sizes[i],
                sizes[i]);
        }
}
```

Figure 10-2. *Output from Listing 10-10*

Let's walk through what's happening in this example. First, we are setting the background color to be white inside the draw function. Also, we are calling the noFill function that would draw the shapes without a fill color. These are just stylistic choices. We are creating an empty sizes array that we will populate with random numbers. Then we are creating a loop that will iterate for 100 times. Inside that loop, for each iteration, we are creating a random value in between 5 and 500 using the random function, and we are pushing that generated random value inside the sizes array using the push method.

The next step remains the same. We are creating ellipses for all the values that exist in the sizes array. Notice how changing a single value in this program, the amount of random numbers being generated, which is at 100 right now, controls the entire outcome. This is a great example that exhibits how simple programming structures can create very robust and scalable solutions.

Using Arrays

Let's work on another visualization using Arrays! The plan is to create an animation that is sequentially and continuously going to display the given words in a stylistic manner.

First, let's refresh our knowledge on how to create text in p5.js. We will be using the text function that takes three arguments: the text to display, and the x and y positions of that text. Using this knowledge, let's just display the word "JavaScript" on the screen on a light-colored background (see Listing 10-11 and Figure 10-3).

Listing 10-11. Using the text fucntion

```
function setup() {
        createCanvas(800, 300);
}
```

```
function draw() {
        background(200);
        text('JavaScript', width/2, height/2);
}
```

Figure 10-3. *Output from Listing 10-11*

Notice that the text we created is not vertically aligned. It doesn't look centered. It is easy to fix this using a function called textAlign in p5.js (Listing 10-12). Just call this function inside the setup function by passing the value CENTER to it. This will take care of the vertical alignment. We could pass CENTER to this function one more time to horizontally align the text as well.

Listing 10-12. Using the textAlign function

```
textAlign(CENTER, CENTER);
```

Next, let's format the text so that it would look a bit better. In Listing 10-13, we set the text size to 45 pixels by using the textSize function and made the text color white using the fill function (see Figure 10-4 for the results).

Listing 10-13. Using textAlign and styling the text

```
function setup() {
        createCanvas(800, 300);
        textAlign(CENTER, CENTER); // centering the text
}

function draw() {
        background(200);
        fill(255); // text color
        textSize(45); // text size
        text('JavaScript', width/2, height/2);
}
```

Figure 10-4. Output for Listing 10-13

Perfect! In this example, we would like to create an array of words and continuously cycle through them. Let's first create the array that we will be using. We will be creating it outside the draw function because we only need to create this array once. If we were to declare it inside the draw function, then it would continuously be created and destroyed with each call to the draw function (which happens around 60 times a second by default!).

Let's create a variable called words outside the draw and setup functions (Listing 10-14). Since the variable is initialized outside of both the setup and draw functions, it can be used from both of them.

Listing 10-14. Creating a words variable

```
var words = ['I', 'love', 'programming', 'with', 'JavaScript'];
```

Next, we need to devise a way that will continuously generate a value in between 0 and the length of this array to be able to refer to the individual items in an array. To do so, we can use the remainder (%) operator.

Using the `remainder` Operator

The remainder operator is a bit different than all the operators we have seen previously, such as plus or minus, so it might be beneficial to see how it works. Given two values, the remainder operator returns the remainder left over when the first value is divided by the second value. The % operator symbolizes it.

As we can see in Listing 10-15, given an incrementally increasing first value, the remainder operator allows us to cycle through the second value minus one.

Listing 10-15. Remainder operator

```
console.log(1 % 6) // returns 1.
console.log(2 % 6) // returns 2.
console.log(3 % 6) // returns 3.
console.log(4 % 6) // returns 4.
console.log(5 % 6) // returns 5.
console.log(6 % 6) // returns 0.
console.log(7 % 6) // returns 1.
// etc..
```

You might find yourself thinking: "how would you even know this?" As in, this can be something that is really hard to think of, if all we knew was what the `remainder` operator did but didn't have any practice using it. This is perfectly normal. You get to understand what kind of an operator or structure you can use for a certain purpose by seeing other people use it. It is sometimes a matter of experience and practice rather than knowledge.

If I am to provide a constant supply of incremental values to a `remainder` operator alongside with the length of my array, I will be able to generate values cycling in between 0 and that length.

In the p5.js context, that constant supply of values could be the `frameCount` variable. Remember `frameCount` tells us how many times the `draw` function has been called so far. As shown in Listing 10-16, let's create a variable inside the `draw` function with the name `currentIndex`, which uses the `remainder` operator, the `frameCount` p5.js variable and the length of the words array to create values in between 0 and the length of the array minus one.

Listing 10-16. Using the remainder operator

```
var currentIndex = frameCount % words.length;
```

We can `console.log` this statement to verify we are indeed creating values in the desired range. But a better way of doing things might be just to use the `text` function that we already have to display this value using p5.js. We are visual learners after all.

One thing to notice at this point is that the display of the numbers is simply too fast; it is really hard to understand what's going on. We should slow p5.js down or else our text will be very hard to read. One way of doing it could be to decrease the frame rate using the `frameRate` function. As shown in Listing 10-17, let's change the `frameRate` value inside the setup function to 3. See the results in Figure 10-5.

Listing 10-17. Slowing down the frameRate

```
var words = ['I', 'love', 'programming', 'with', 'JavaScript'];

function setup() {
        createCanvas(800, 300);
        textAlign(CENTER, CENTER);
        frameRate(3); // using a lower frame rate to slowdown
        the text
}

function draw() {
        var currentIndex = frameCount % words.length;
        background(200);
        fill(255);
        textSize(45);
        text(currentIndex, width/2, height/2);
}
```

Figure 10-5. *Output from Listing 10-17*

Awesome! Using this code we should be able to see a range of numbers being displayed on the screen. But we are not interested in displaying numbers to the screen – but the words inside the array. That's very easy to do using our knowledge. We will use the square bracket notation to access individual items inside the array.

As shown in Listing 10-18, let's create another variable called currentWord. This variable will store the current word as determined by the currentIndex variable. Now we can use this variable instead of currentIndex inside the text function.

Listing 10-18. Creating variable currentWord

```
var currentWord = words[currentIndex];
```

We are almost done. But one another thing that I would like to do is to change the background color per word since this is not aesthetically pleasing at all right now.

We will create another array called colors that will contain color information. It turns out that we can pass an array into p5.js color functions, and it is the same as passing values one by one to it.

So, as shown in Listing 10-19, these two expressions will create the same color as each other.

Listing 10-19. Using an array as a value for the fill function

```
fill(255, 0, 0);
fill([255, 0, 0]);
```

We will create the colors array that contains arrays of colors we will use. We can try to come up with color values by ourselves, but it is hard to find good-looking colors that way.

Adobe has a web page called Adobe Color CC (https://color.adobe.com) where we can find color themes to use in our designs. I will use it to find a theme that will go with my visualization.

Under the explore tab in Adobe Color CC, you can select a desirable theme. Hover over your desired theme and click "Edit Copy." This will lead you to a page where you can see the RGB values for the colors. Listing 10-20 is a sample of colors picked from that website.

Listing 10-20. Color samples from Adobe Color CC

```
var colors = [
        [63, 184, 175],
        [127, 199, 175],
        [218, 216, 167],
        [255, 158, 157],
        [255, 61, 127],
];
```

Notice my formatting for the data is a bit different because I didn't want the line length to be too long as it might hamper the legibility of our code. This is just a stylistic choice.

Now we can use these color values inside the fill function to change the color of the background with each frame. Listing 10-21 shows what the final code looks like.

Listing 10-21. Final Code

```
var words = ['I', 'love', 'programming', 'with', 'JavaScript'];
var colors = [
        [63, 184, 175],
        [127, 199, 175],
        [218, 216, 167],
        [255, 158, 157],
        [255, 61, 127],
];

function setup() {
        createCanvas(800, 300);
        textAlign(CENTER, CENTER);
        frameRate(3); // using a lower frame rate to slowdown
        the text
}
```

```
function draw() {
        var currentIndex = frameCount % words.length;
        var currentColor = colors[currentIndex];
        var currentWord = words[currentIndex];
        background(currentColor);
        fill(255);
        textSize(45);
        text(currentWord, width / 2, height / 2);
}
```

Summary

In this chapter we learned about a JavaScript data structure called Arrays. Arrays allow us to store multiple values of any type in a sequential fashion. The values stored in an array can be accessed using the square bracket notation.

We can populate an array with the desired values when they are first created or after their creation, using the push method. Arrays are particularly useful when used with loops. Loops let us access the items in an array in a very easy manner.

We also learned about the remainder operator. A remainder operator returns the remainder from a division operation in between two numbers. Using this operator, we can derive sequential values that cycle in between zero and the desired value.

Practice

Build a function called countdown that will get two arguments – a number and a message – (Listing 10-22) and will create a visualization that is similar to the one above, which will display a countdown from the given number to the number 0. At the end of the countdown, it should display the given message, the second argument, to the screen.

Feel free to add another parameter to the function that will control how long each number will stay on the screen.

Listing 10-22.

```
countdown(10, "Launch!");
```

CHAPTER 11

Events

In Chapter 6, we learned about a p5.js variable called `mouseIsPressed`, which assumes the value to be `true` while the mouse is being pressed and `false` for all other instances.

We also learned that this is not a great way of capturing user input as the execution speed of the `draw` function can make it hard to get this variable updated in a reliable way. In this chapter we'll review other ways of handling user input inside p5.js, namely, the *events*, which solve this problem. Using events, we can capture the user input outside the `draw` function loop.

There are numerous event functions in p5.js that we can declare to make use of the event system. Here we'll focus on two event functions: the `mousePressed` and `keyPressed` event functions.

Using mousePressed

The idea is similar to the `draw` and `setup` functions where we declare this function with this particular name, which is treated by p5.js in a special manner (just like `setup` and `draw` functions are).

In a p5.js code, the function we declare under the name `mousePressed` gets triggered every time the mouse buttons are pressed. Let's rewrite our previous example that makes use of the `mouseIsPressed` variable to make use of the `mousePressed` event function instead (Listing 11-1).

© Engin Arslan 2018
E. Arslan, *Learn JavaScript with p5.js*, https://doi.org/10.1007/978-1-4842-3426-6_11

Listing 11-1. Using mousePressed event function

```
var toggle = true;

function setup() {
      createCanvas(800, 300);
      rectMode(CENTER);
}

function draw() {
      // display a different bg color based on the toggle
      value
      if (toggle === true) {
            background(1, 186, 240);
      } else {
            background(250, 150, 50);
      }

      // declaration of variables
      var x = width / 2;
      var y = height / 2;
      var size = 200;

      if (frameCount < 60) {
            size = size + frameCount;
      } else {
            size = size + 60;
      }

      // circle
      fill(237, 34, 93);
      noStroke();
      ellipse(x, y, size, size);
```

```
      // rectangle
      fill(255);
      rect(x, y, size*0.75, size*0.15);
}

function mousePressed() {
      toggle = !toggle; // change the toggle value to be
                              opposite.
}
```

Well, that was a simple refactor! We are simply declaring a function we don't execute ourselves. The execution is handled by p5.js whenever the corresponding action takes place.

There are lots of other event functions. A complete list can be found at `https://p5js.org/reference/#group-Events`.

Using keyPressed

One other event function worth learning about is the keyPressed function. As the name implies, the keyPressed function gets triggered every time a key is pressed. In Listing 11-2, let's quickly test how it works in a brand new sketch.

Listing 11-2. Using the keyPressed function

```
function setup() {
      createCanvas(800, 300);
}

function draw() {
      background(220);
}
```

```
function keyPressed() {
        console.log('pressed');
}
```

In this example, every time we press a key, we will see a message 'pressed' displayed in the console. In Listing 11-3, let's look at a more involved example where pressing a key each time creates a shape in the canvas.

Listing 11-3. Drawing a shape with every keypress

```
var pressed;

function setup() {
        createCanvas(800, 300);
        background(220);
}

function draw() {
        if (pressed === true) {
            ellipse(
                    random(width),
                    random(height),
                    50,
                    50
            );
        }
        pressed = false;
}

function keyPressed() {
        pressed = true;
}
```

The shapes are created after we press a key (Figure 11-1).

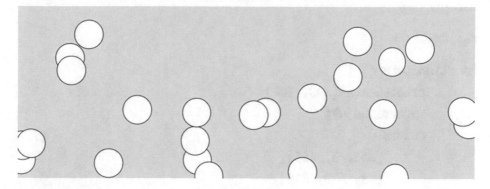

Figure 11-1. *Output from Listing 11-3*

Notice a couple of things. First of all, we moved the background function to be under the setup function. This is to ensure that the shapes we draw remain on the screen. If we are to have a background function called inside the draw function, then it would paint over everything, on every frame which is not desirable for this use case. Also, we are spreading the ellipse function call over a couple of lines, again, to increase legibility.

We have a global variable called pressed. With each keypress, we are setting the value of this global variable to be true. When this happens, the draw function renders an ellipse to the screen since the conditional statement gets executed. Then the draw function immediately sets the pressed value to false again so that we only get one ellipse.

In Listing 11-4, we will improve this example a little bit to make it more pleasing to the eye. Currently, the circles are looking a bit too uniform, and the colors are a bit too dull. We will make it so that every time we are creating a circle, it uses a random size between 0 and 200 and a random color from a list of predefined random colors (Figure 11-2).

Listing 11-4. Changing size and color

```
var pressed;

var colors = [];

function setup() {
        createCanvas(800, 300);
        background(0);
        colors = [
                [245, 3, 155],
                [13, 159, 215],
                [148, 177, 191],
                [100, 189, 167],
                [242, 226, 133],
                [176, 230, 110],
                [123, 90, 240]
        ];
}

function draw() {
        noStroke();
        if (pressed === true) {
                var randomIndex = parseInt(random(colors.length), 10);
                // convert the given number to an integer
                var randomSize = random(200);

                fill(colors[randomIndex]);
                ellipse(
                        random(width),
                        random(height),
                        randomSize,
                        randomSize
                );
```

```
    }
    pressed = false;
}

function keyPressed() {
    pressed = true;
}
```

Figure 11-2. *Output from Listing 11-4*

To be able to select a random color each time a key is pressed, we need to generate a random integer in between 0 and the length of the colors array minus 1. We use minus 1 because array indices start counting from 0.

To generate any random number in between 0 and the length of the array minus 1, we can simply write the random function as random(colors.length). This will end up generating a number in between 0 and up until the number of items in the colors array (excluding that number). The problem, though, is that the number being generated is a floating-point number, meaning it has decimal places. However, we need an integer number to be able to access items in an array. So we need to convert the decimal number into a whole number. There are a couple of ways to solve this. One way could be to use the p5.js floor function, which rounds down the given floating-point number to the nearest integer. Another solution could be to use the native JavaScript function called parseInt, which converts a given value into an integer - if the value can be converted. We can't expect to throw a string name value to it and receive an integer.

As shown in Listing 11-5, we need to pass a second parameter to parseInt function to set the number base that the calculation will happen. That base almost always is 10. Using the parseInt function on a float number looks something like this.

Listing 11-5. Using parseInt on a float number

```
var num = parseInt(0.5, 10);
console.log(num); // will be 0.
```

Identifying the pressed key is only part of the issue, though. Another thing that we should be able to do is to identify which button the user pressed. Inside the keyPressed function, we could theoretically identify any key pressed by using the keyCode variable. A keyCode variable holds the last key that the user pressed in an encoded manner, such that if the user pressed the key 'a', it would return the value '65', for 'b'; '66', etc...

Since p5.js is a helpful library, this makes it easier to identify some of the keys by providing predefined variables for them, like: BACKSPACE, DELETE, ENTER, RETURN, TAB, ESCAPE, SHIFT, CONTROL, OPTION, ALT, UP_ARROW, DOWN_ARROW, LEFT_ARROW, RIGHT_ARROW.

For example, Listing 11-6 provides a small code snippet that executes a console.log statement whenever the 'Enter' key is pressed.

Listing 11-6. Using keyCode values

```
function setup() {
        createCanvas(800, 300);
}

function draw() {
        background(220);
}
```

```
function keyPressed() {
        if (keyCode === ENTER) {
                console.log('Enter Pressed');
        }
}
```

Using the keyCode variable, we could identify which alphanumeric key is pressed with a bit of decoding. But there is another variable that works specifically well for the alphanumeric characters and that is called key. The key variable stores the value of the alphanumeric key that is pressed as is, so it makes it easier to identify which key was pressed.

Summary

In this chapter, we learned about a better way to handle events, and that is event functions. We focused specifically on two event functions: the mousePressed and keyPressed event functions.

We also learned about some of the variables we can use inside the keyPressed function: key and keyCode. Using key makes identifying the alphanumeric keypresses easier whereas keyCode is ideal for detecting other keypresses as it can be compared against p5.js variables such as ENTER, SPACE, etc. That makes identifying those buttons easier.

From the JavaScript part of the things, we learned about the parseInt function that can be used to convert number-like values (which include strings that represent a number as well) into an integer number.

Practice

Draw a rectangle to the screen where the keyboard arrow keys can control the position of the rectangle.

CHAPTER 12

More on p5.js

At this point, we are almost ready to work on our final project: an interactive game built using JavaScript and p5.js! That's in the next chapter. Before we do that, I would like to demonstrate a couple of more useful p5.js functions to extend the realm of things we can build.

Have you noticed how we can draw shapes on the screen using our current knowledge, but we can't really transform them such as rotating them around their center? That's a big blocker on the kinds of visuals we can build, so in this chapter let's learn how to do transformations in p5.js to enhance our abilities.

Rotate and Translate

Having used other kinds of drawing libraries, I should say that doing transformations such as scaling, rotating, and translating shapes can be a bit unintuitive in p5.js. Listings 12-1 and 12-2 are examples demonstrating how to use the p5.js rotate function, which allows us to rotate shapes.

Listing 12-1. Drawing rectangles without rotation

```
function setup() {
      createCanvas(800, 300);
      rectMode(CENTER);
      noStroke();
}
```

```
function draw() {
      background(220);
      fill(237, 34, 93);
      rect(width/2, height/2, 50, 50);
      rect(width/2+50, height/2+50, 50, 50);
}
```

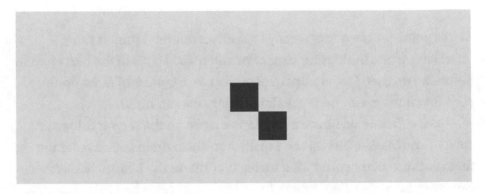

Figure 12-1. *Output for Listing 12-1*

Currently, we are drawing two rectangles that are diagonal to each other (Figure 12-1). Let's make use of the rotate function to see what's going to happen.

Listing 12-2. Using the rotate function

```
function setup() {
      createCanvas(800, 300);
      rectMode(CENTER);
      noStroke();
}

function draw() {
      background(220);
      fill(237, 34, 93);
      rotate(5);
```

```
    rect(width/2, height/2, 50, 50);
    rect(width/2+50, height/2+50, 50, 50);
}
```

You will notice that both of the shapes disappeared from the screen. If you were expecting the shapes to move by only 5 degrees, this must be a confusing result. This happens because the default units that rotate function work within p5.js are radians. We can make this function work using degrees instead by using the angleMode function with the DEGREES p5.js variable. As shown in Listing 12-3, make this declaration inside the setup function.

Listing 12-3. Using angleMode

```
angleMode(DEGREES);
```

Now things work in a way that is more or less expected. We can now observe that when we call the rotate function, we end up rotating every shape that comes after the function call (Listing 12-4 and Figure 12-2).

Listing 12-4. Using rotate with angleMode

```
function setup() {
    createCanvas(800, 300);
    rectMode(CENTER);
    noStroke();
    angleMode(DEGREES);
}

function draw() {
    background(220);
    fill(237, 34, 93);
    rotate(5);
    rect(width/2, height/2, 50, 50);
    rect(width/2+50, height/2+50, 50, 50);
}
```

Figure 12-2. *Output from Listing 12-4*

Another thing to notice is that the rotation happens around the origin point, the top-left corner of the canvas. However, when we control shapes, we usually like to have them rotate around their origin. So this function, as is, doesn't seem to be extremely useful.

To have better control over the rotate function, we should look into the translate function. The translate function moves the object for the given x and y translation amount from the origin point. In Listing 12-5, let's make use of it inside our current setup. See Figure 12-3 for the results.

Listing 12-5. Using the translate function

```
function setup() {
        createCanvas(800, 300);
        rectMode(CENTER);
        noStroke();
        angleMode(DEGREES);
}

function draw() {
        background(220);
        fill(237, 34, 93);
        translate(150, 0); // using translate function
```

```
    rotate(5);
    rect(width/2, height/2, 50, 50);
    rect(width/2+50, height/2+50, 50, 50);
}
```

Figure 12-3. *Output from Listing 12-5*

What's happening right now is that the translate function moves everything inside the canvas 150 pixels to the right. It moves the entire coordinate system as the rotation is also happening around the 150px right-hand side of the origin instead of happening from the origin.

Without further ado, Listing 12-6 and Figure 12-4 are about how to rotate things around their origin. I think it is easier to show how it is done than to explain it. We will work with a single shape for now.

Listing 12-6. Rotating around the origin

```
function setup() {
    createCanvas(800, 300);
    rectMode(CENTER);
    noStroke();
    angleMode(DEGREES);
}
```

```
function draw() {
      background(220);
      fill(237, 34, 93);

      // rotating the shape around it's origin
      translate(width/2, height/2);
      rotate(45);
      rect(0, 0, 100, 100);
}
```

Figure 12-4. *Output from Listing 12-6*

In this example, we are drawing a shape as usual, but using the translation function to set its x and y coordinates instead of feeding those values directly into the shape drawing function. Doing this, when coupled with using the rectMode function, allows us to draw the shape with its center located at the origin. Basically, we start off by drawing the shape at the origin point as all the transformation functions work relative to that point. Then we use the translate and rotate functions to move the shape to the desired position and angle. Using this approach, we need to remember to call the rotate after the translate function or the rotation will still happen relative to the original origin point, which is probably not desired.

The current shortcoming with this approach and with the usage of transformation functions, in general, is that everything we draw from this point onward will be using this new origin point. The way to fix this is by using the push and pop functions.

Push and Pop

The p5.js push function allows us to create a new state and the pop function restores the state to the previous conditions. This allows us to have completely different settings applied to individual objects without worrying if those settings will affect the shapes that come after, as long as we do everything in between a push and a pop call. Again it is easier to see this in an example (Listing 12-7 and Figure 12-5).

With our current setup, everything we draw after the translate and rotate functions will have that 45 degrees of rotation applied to them.

Listing 12-7. Translate function with multiple shapes

```
function setup() {
      createCanvas(800, 300);
      rectMode(CENTER);
      noStroke();
      angleMode(DEGREES);
}

function draw() {
      background(220);

      translate(width/2, height/2);
      rotate(45);
```

```
    // pink rectangle
    fill(237, 34, 93);
    rect(0, 0, 150, 150);

    // white rectangle
    fill(255, 255, 255);
    rect(0, 0, 75, 75);
}
```

Fgure 12-5. *Output from Listing 12-7*

In Listing 12-8, let's implement the push and pop functions here so that we can isolate the transformation we are applying to the larger rectangle. See Figure 12-6 for results.

Listing 12-8. Using the push and pop functions

```
function setup() {
    createCanvas(800, 300);
    rectMode(CENTER);
    noStroke();
    angleMode(DEGREES);
}
```

```
function draw() {
     background(220);

     // translation and rotation will be contained in between
     // push and pop function calls.
     push();
     translate(width/2, height/2);
     rotate(45);
     // pink rectangle
     fill(237, 34, 93);
     rect(0, 0, 150, 150);
     pop();

     // white rectangle
     fill(255, 255, 255);
     rect(0, 0, 75, 75);
}
```

Figure 12-6. *Output for Listing 12-8*

Brilliant! Whatever we are doing in between the push and pop functions don't end up affecting anything else outside these function calls. It is important to note that we will always call the push and pop functions together. Using one but not the other doesn't make any sense.

In Listing 12-9, let's update our example so that we can still translate the pink rectangle to the middle but apply a different rotation value to it.

Listing 12-9. Applying different translations to different shapes

```
function setup() {
        createCanvas(800, 300);
        rectMode(CENTER);
        noStroke();
        angleMode(DEGREES);
}

function draw() {
        background(220);

        push();
        translate(width/2, height/2);
        rotate(45);
        // pink rectangle
        fill(237, 34, 93);
        rect(0, 0, 150, 150);
        pop();

        push();
        translate(width/2, height/2);
        rotate(30);
        // white rectangle
        fill(255, 255, 255);
        rect(0, 0, 75, 75);
        pop();
}
```

If you find yourself wishing that p5.js transformations weren't this complicated, you can try building your own functions to handle and abstract away the complexity. Listing 12-10 provides an example rectangle function that takes a fifth argument, which is the rotation parameter.

Listing 12-10. Declaring a custom function to handle transformations

```
function rectC(x, y, width, height, rotation) {
      if (rotation === undefined) {
            rotation = 0;
      }
      push();
      translate(x, y);
      rotate(rotation);
      rect(0, 0, width, height);
      pop();
}
```

Here, we are creating our rectangle drawing function called rectC that wraps the original rect function but uses the push and pop internally to save state and set transformations, and it accepts an optional rotation parameter. If the rotation argument is not provided, then it will assume the value is undefined. If that's the case, I can just set the rotation value to be 0 instead. Listing 12-11 is the previous example refactored to make use of this function. Notice it is much more concise this time.

Listing 12-11. Using a custom function to handle transformations

```
function setup() {
      createCanvas(800, 300);
      rectMode(CENTER);
      noStroke();
      angleMode(DEGREES);
}
```

```
function draw() {
      background(220);

      // pink rectangle
      fill(237, 34, 93);
      rectC(width/2, height/2, 150, 150, 45);

      // white rectangle
      fill(255, 255, 255);
      rectC(width/2, height/2, 75, 75, 30);
}

function rectC(x, y, width, height, rotation) {
      // if rotation value is not provided assume it is 0
      if (rotation === undefined) {
            rotation = 0;
      }
      push();
      translate(x, y);
      rotate(rotation);
      rect(0, 0, width, height);
      pop();
}
```

Summary

When working with a drawing library, it becomes pretty important to be able to transform shapes. In this chapter, we saw how the p5.js transform functions work. We learned about the translate and rotate functions. We also learned about the angleMode function, which lets us set the units used by the rotate function.

We then learned about the push and pop functions and found out how they can be used in conjunction with the transformation functions to isolate the state and apply transformations to individual shapes. While these functions aren't crucial to learning JavaScript, I find that knowing about them is pretty essential when using p5.js.

Practice

Try building something cool on your own before moving on to the next chapter where we will be building an interactive game together!

CHAPTER 13

Final Project

In this chapter, we will be building a game that makes use of everything that we have seen so far. We will also learn a couple of more tricks along the way as well. The fact that we can build a simple game using the p5.js library is pretty impressive and very illustrative of the capabilities of this library.

Our game is going to be simple. It is a typing speed game where we will be rapidly displaying numbers to the player and expect the player to enter the current number on the screen using their keyboard. If they enter the correct number in the given amount of time, they score. We will keep track of the score to be able to display it at the end of the game. It would be great if the game presents a strong visual experience, but the primary focus is going to be around getting the game logic right.

Let's create a breakdown of things that we need to create:

- We need to display a number on the screen every N frames.

- We don't want the number to remain static on the screen. It should be animated to make it easier or harder to read with time.

- That number needs to remain on the screen until the next number is displayed or until the player presses a key in an attempt to match the number.

- If the player entry matches the number on the screen, we will display a success message. If not, the failure will be indicated.

© Engin Arslan 2018
E. Arslan, *Learn JavaScript with p5.js*, https://doi.org/10.1007/978-1-4842-3426-6_13

- We need to keep track of the amount of success and failure. After X many frames or attempts, display the results to the user.

- We need to find a way to restart the game after it is over.

Getting Started

The first item on our list is to be able to display a unique number on the screen at regular intervals. Remember that we used the `remainder` operator (%) to achieve this feat before. Here, we will be displaying a number in between 0 and 9 on the screen every 100 frames (Listing 13-1).

Listing 13-1. Displaying a random integer every 100 frames

```
var content;

function setup() {
        createCanvas(800, 300);
        textAlign(CENTER, CENTER);
}

function draw() {
        background(220);

        if (frameCount === 1 || frameCount % 100 === 0) {
                content = parseInt(random(10), 10);
        }

        text(content, width/2, height/2);
}
```

In this example, we are first initializing a variable called `content` in the global scope. Then in the `draw` function, we are using the `random` function to generate a random number on the first frame or every 100 frames and then save that value inside the content variable. However, the problem with the random function is that it returns a floating-point number. We would like to have whole numbers, integers, for the purpose of this game. So we are using the parseInt function to convert the floating-point number to an integer number. Remember that the parseInt function requires you to pass the second argument to set the base for the numerical system of the operation, which is almost always going to be the number 10 for common use cases.

We are storing the generated number inside a variable called content and then passing that variable into a text function that displays it in the middle of the screen.

We will need lots of custom behavior from the number that we will display on the screen; so we will create a JavaScript object to represent it. This way, the functions we create to manipulate the number (such as transformation operations, color configurations, etc.) can remain grouped under the object that helps with the organization of the program. We will call this new object GuessItem. I am well aware that's a terrible name but as they say, there are two hard things in computer science: *cache invalidation, naming things, and off-by-one errors.*

If we are to look at our code after this attempt at creating a JavaScript object that wraps the p5.js text function, it might look like we are adding additional complexity for no reason, as our code grew almost twice in size. But containing the text drawing functionality under an object will help with organizing our code a lot down the road. See Listing 13-2.

Listing 13-2. Text drawing functionality

```
var guessItem;

function setup() {
        createCanvas(800, 300);
}
```

```
function draw() {
        if (frameCount === 1 || frameCount % 100 === 0) {
                background(220);
                guessItem = new GuessItem(width/2, height/2, 1);
        }

        guessItem.render();
}

function GuessItem(x, y, scl) {
        this.x = x;
        this.y = y;
        this.scale = scl;
        this.content = getContent();

        function getContent() {
                // generate a random integer in between 0 and 9
                return parseInt(random(10), 10);
        }

        this.render = function () {
                push();
                textAlign(CENTER, CENTER);
                translate(this.x, this.y);
                scale(this.scale);
                text(this.content, 0, 0);
                pop();
        }
}
```

Let's focus on the GuessItem object first. GuessItem is an object-creating Constructor Function that requires three arguments: the x and y position and the scale of the shape that it draws to the screen. It also has two methods on itself. One of them is getContent, which generates a random number in between 0 and 10 and stores it inside a property called content. Another method it contains is render, which displays the content property of a GuessItem object instance on the screen.

Every operation inside the render method lives under the push and pop function calls. This allows us to contain the setting and transformation-related state changes that happen inside this method contained in this object. Here, we are using the translate and scale transform functions to change the position and size of the text object. We didn't see the scale function before, but it's a transformation function that is very similar to translate and rotate functions. Just as the name implies, it controls the scale of the drawing area, and it has similar working principles to other transformation functions, so it is best to contain it in between the push and pop functions.

We could have used a textSize function call for the size, but I usually find working with transform functions to be a bit more intuitive.

In Listing 13-3, we will now use this GuessItem constructor function to create an object that draws to the screen. We instantiate a GuessItem object with several parameters on line 10 and save it inside a variable called guessItem.

Listing 13-3. Creating a GuessItem instance

```
guessItem = new GuessItem(width/2, height/2, 1);
```

The number that the GuessItem is going to display is determined at the instantiation as well. Drawing this object to the screen happens on line 13 using the render method it has (Listing 13-4).

Listing 13-4. Using the render method

```
guessItem.render();
```

In Listing 13-5, let's make it so that the text grows in size during its lifetime to add some dynamism to the game.

Listing 13-5. Making the text grow in size

```
var guessItem;

function setup() {
        createCanvas(800, 300);
}

function draw() {
        background(220);
        if (frameCount === 1 || frameCount % 100 === 0) {
                guessItem = new GuessItem(width / 2, height /
                2, 1);
        }

        guessItem.render();
}

function GuessItem(x, y, scl) {
        this.x = x;
        this.y = y;
        this.scale = scl;
        this.scaleIncrement = 1;
        this.content = getContent();

        function getContent() {
                // generate a random integer in between 0 and 9
                return parseInt(random(10), 10);
        }
```

```
    this.render = function() {
            push();
            textAlign(CENTER, CENTER);
            translate(this.x, this.y);
            scale(this.scale);
            text(this.content, 0, 0);
            // increase the scale value by the increment
            value with each render
            this.scale = this.scale + this.scaleIncrement;
            pop();
    }
}
```

We added a way to increment the scale function with each call to the render function (Listing 13-6).

Listing 13-6. Increment the scale function

```
this.scale = this.scale + this.scaleIncrement;
```

We also added a new variable inside the GuessItem constructor function called scaleIncrement that controls the speed of scaling. Play with this value to be able to change the pace of animation. We could, for example, increase this value to make the game harder.

In Listing 13-7, we will add a bit more parameterization to our script to be able to control the way and frequency the numbers are displayed.

Listing 13-7. Controlling the frequency of numbers

```
var guessItem;
// controls the frequency that a new random number is
generated.
var interval = 100;
```

```
function setup() {
        createCanvas(800, 300);
}

function draw() {
        background(220);
        if (frameCount === 1 || frameCount % interval === 0) {
                guessItem = new GuessItem(width / 2,
                height / 2, 1);
        }

        guessItem.render();
}

function GuessItem(x, y, scl) {
        this.x = x;
        this.y = y;
        this.scale = scl;
        this.scaleIncrement = 0.5;
        this.content = getContent();
        this.alpha = 255;
        this.alphaDecrement = 3;

        function getContent() {
                // generate a random integer in between 0 and 9
                return parseInt(random(10), 10);
        }

        this.render = function() {
                push();
                fill(0, this.alpha);
                textAlign(CENTER, CENTER);
                translate(this.x, this.y);
                scale(this.scale);
```

```
        text(this.content, 0, 0);
        // increase the scale value by the increment
        value with each render
        this.scale = this.scale + this.scaleIncrement;
        // decrease the alpha value by the decrement
        value with each render
        this.alpha = this.alpha - this.alphaDecrement;
        pop();
    }
}
```

Here, we have a couple of more small tweaks. We added a fill function
to the render method, and we are now dynamically setting alpha for the
displayed number to get more transparent with each frame. I think that
adds to the dynamism of the game. Set that number to something small
to see things get stressful. We also parameterized the frequency of the
creation of GuessItem using a global variable called interval so that we
can play with the value of that variable to make the game easier or harder.

By the way, can you guess why we named the number-generating
function getContent? That's because after we are done with this game, it
should be a fairly trivial thing to update the game to display words instead
of numbers on the screen. Keeping our function names generic helps a
little bit with the future expansion work that we might want to do for this
game.

So far, we only completed two items from our to-do list, which are
displaying a number on the screen by using a given interval and having
that number animated on the screen to add dynamism to our game. In the
next section, we will handle the player interaction.

User Interaction

We still have the outstanding task of fetching the user input and comparing it to the number on the screen. Let's implement that (Listing 13-8).

Listing 13-8. Fetching and comparing user input

```
var guessItem = null;
// controls the frequency that a new random number is
generated.
var interval = 100;
var solution = null;

function setup() {
        createCanvas(800, 300);
}

function draw() {
        background(220);
        if (frameCount === 1 || frameCount % interval === 0) {
                solution = null;
                guessItem = new GuessItem(width / 2,
                height / 2, 1);
        }

        if (guessItem) {
                guessItem.render();
        }

        if (solution === true) {
                background(255);
        } else if (solution === false) {
                background(0);
        }
}
```

```
function keyPressed() {
        if (guessItem !== null) {
                // check to see if the pressed key matches to
                the displayed number.
                // if so set the solution global variable to a
                corresponding value.
                console.log('you pressed: ', key);
                solution = guessItem.solve(key);
                console.log(solution)
                guessItem = null;
        } else {
                console.log('nothing to be solved');
        }
}

function GuessItem(x, y, scl) {
        this.x = x;
        this.y = y;
        this.scale = scl;
        this.scaleIncrement = 0.5;
        this.content = getContent();
        this.alpha = 255;
        this.alphaDecrement = 3;
        this.solved = null;

        function getContent() {
                // generate a random integer in between 0 and 9
                return parseInt(random(10), 10);
        }
```

```javascript
this.solve = function(input) {
        // check to see if the given input is
        equivalent to the content.
        // set solved to the corresponding value.
        var solved;
        if (input === this.content) {
                solved = true;
        } else {
                solved = false;
        }
        this.solved = solved;
        return solved;
}

this.render = function() {
        push();
        if (this.solved === false) {
                return;
        }
        fill(0, this.alpha);
        textAlign(CENTER, CENTER);
        translate(this.x, this.y);
        scale(this.scale);
        text(this.content, 0, 0);
        // increase the scale value by the increment
        value with each render
        this.scale = this.scale + this.scaleIncrement;
        // decrease the alpha value by the decrement
        value with each render
        this.alpha = this.alpha - this.alphaDecrement;
        pop();
    }
}
```

We updated the code in a bunch of places. To be able to achieve our task, we implemented a new method on the GuessItem object called solve. The solve method gets a user input and returns either true or false depending if the given user input matches to the GuessItem content variable. We end up saving the result inside a solution global variable (Listing 13-9).

Listing 13-9. Solve method inside the GuessItem

```
this.solve = function(input) {
        // check to see if the given input is equivalent to the
        content.
        // set solved to the corresponding value.
        var solved;
        if (input === this.content) {
                solved = true;
        } else {
                solved = false;
        }
        this.solved = solved;
        return solved;
}
```

To be able to get user input, we created a p5.js event function, keyPressed, which is called every time the user presses a key. Inside this keyPressed function we call the solve method of a guessItem object to see if the pressed key matches the content of the guessItem. If so, the solution variable will be true, and if not, it would be false.

Listing 13-10. Handling key press

```
function keyPressed() {
                // check to see if the pressed key matches to
                the displayed number.
```

```
                        // if so set the solution global variable to a
                        corresponding value.
            if (guessItem !== null) {
                        console.log('you pressed: ', key);
                        solution = guessItem.solve(key);
                        console.log(solution)
                        guessItem = null;
            } else {
                        console.log('nothing to be solved');
            }
}
```

We are only reading the keypresses from the player if there is a
GuessItem that exists. That's because we are now assigning a null to the
guessItem variable once the player makes a guess. Doing so effectively gets
rid of the current guessItem object. That allows us to prevent the player
from making multiple guesses for a number. Since the guessItem variable
can now have a null variable, meaning there might not be a guess item
present in the game because the user tried to guess its value, our call to the
render method might fail. To prevent that from happening, we are putting
that render call inside a conditional. Additionally, we have a couple of
console.log functions inside the keyPressed function to have a sense of
what's going on by looking at the console messages.

As a testing measure, we have added a conditional that changes the
background color to black if the player guess is wrong and to white, if it is
correct using the solution variable.

Having said all that, this code doesn't work right now. Even our correct
guesses are turning the screen to black. Can you guess why?

It turns out the reason is that the keyPressed function captures
the pressed keys as *strings* whereas the generated content inside the
GuessItem object is a *number*. Using triple equal signs, ===, we are looking
to see if there is strict equality in between these two values, and there is

none. That is because a number is never equal to a string. So, our function returns false. To be able to fix this issue, we are going to convert the number generated into a string by using the JavaScript function String (Listing 13-11).

Listing 13-11. Converting the random integer to a string

```
function getContent() {
        return String(parseInt(random(10), 10));
}
```

Keeping the User Score

To be able to give feedback to the user as to how they are doing in the game, we will start storing their scores. We will make use of this stored data to make the game stop after a set amount of guesses or losses (Listing 13-12).

Listing 13-12. Storing scores

```
var guessItem = null;
// controls the frequency that a new random number is
generated.
var interval = 100;
// an array to store solution values
var results = [];
var solution = null;

function setup() {
        createCanvas(800, 300);
}
```

```
function draw() {
        background(220);
        if (frameCount === 1 || frameCount % interval === 0) {
                solution = null;
                guessItem = new GuessItem(width/2, height/2, 1);
        }

        if (guessItem) {
                guessItem.render();
        }

        if (solution === true) {
                background(255);
        } else if (solution === false) {
                background(0);
        }
}

function keyPressed() {
        if (guessItem !== null) {
                // check to see if the pressed key matches to
                the displayed number.
                // if so set the solution global variable to a
                corresponding value.
                console.log('you pressed: ', key);
                solution = guessItem.solve(key);
                console.log(solution);
                if (solution) {
                        results.push(true);
                } else {
                        results.push(false);
                }
                guessItem = null;
```

```
        } else {
                console.log('nothing to be solved');
        }
}

function GuessItem(x, y, scl) {
        this.x = x;
        this.y = y;
        this.scale = scl;
        this.scaleIncrement = 0.5;
        this.content = getContent();
        this.alpha = 255;
        this.alphaDecrement = 3;
        this.solved = null;

        function getContent() {
                // generate a random integer in between 0 and 9
                return String(parseInt(random(10), 10));
        }

        this.solve = function(input) {
                // check to see if the given input is
                equivalent to the content.
                // set solved to the corresponding value.
                var solved;
                if (input === this.content) {
                        solved = true;
                } else {
                        solved = false;
                }
                this.solved = solved;
                return solved;
        }
```

```
        this.render = function () {
                push();
                if (this.solved === false) {
                        return;
                }
                fill(0, this.alpha);
                textAlign(CENTER, CENTER);
                translate(this.x, this.y);
                scale(this.scale);
                text(this.content, 0, 0);
                // increase the scale value by the increment
                value with each render
                this.scale = this.scale + this.scaleIncrement;
                // decrease the alpha value by the decrement
                value with each render
                this.alpha = this.alpha - this.alphaDecrement;
                pop();
        }
}
```

In Listing 13-13, we created a results array to be able to store the player score. Every time the player makes a correct guess, we push a true value in there; and every time the player makes a wrong guess, we push a false.

Listing 13-13. Creating a results array

```
if (solution) {
        results.push(true);
} else {
        results.push(false);
}
```

We should also build some functionality to get the value of the `results` array and evaluate it. For that purpose, we will build a function called getGameScore (Listing 13-14). It will get the `results` array and evaluate it to see what the current user score is.

Listing 13-14. Building a getGameScore function

```
var guessItem = null;
// controls the frequency that a new random number is generated
var interval = 100;
// an array to store solution values
var results = [];
var solution = null;

function setup() {
        createCanvas(800, 300);
}

function draw() {
        // if there are 3 losses or 10 attempts stop the game
        var gameScore = getGameScore(results);
        if (gameScore.loss === 3 || gameScore.total === 10) {
                return;
        }
        background(220);
        if (frameCount === 1 || frameCount % interval === 0) {
                solution = null;
                guessItem = new GuessItem(width/2, height/2, 1);
        }

        if (guessItem) {
                guessItem.render();
        }
```

```
        if (solution === true) {
                background(255);
        } else if (solution === false) {
                background(0);
        }
}

function getGameScore(score) {
        // given a score array, calculate the number of wins
        and losses.
        var wins = 0;
        var losses = 0;
        var total = score.length;

        for (var i = 0; i < total; i++) {
                var item = score[i];
                if (item === true) {
                        wins = wins+1;
                } else {
                        losses = losses+1;
                }
        }

        return {win: wins, loss: losses, total: total};
}

function keyPressed() {
        if (guessItem !== null) {
                // check to see if the pressed key matches to
                the displayed number.
                // if so set the solution global variable to a
                corresponding value.
                console.log('you pressed: ', key);
```

```
            solution = guessItem.solve(key);
            console.log(solution);
            if (solution) {
                    results.push(true);
            } else {
                    results.push(false);
            }
            guessItem = null;
    } else {
            console.log('nothing to be solved');
    }
}

function GuessItem(x, y, scl) {
        this.x = x;
        this.y = y;
        this.scale = scl;
        this.scaleIncrement = 0.5;
        this.content = getContent();
        this.alpha = 255;
        this.alphaDecrement = 3;
        this.solved;

        function getContent() {
                // generate a random integer in between 0 and 9
                return String(parseInt(random(10), 10));
        }

        this.solve = function(input) {
                // check to see if the given input is
                equivalent to the content.
                // set solved to the corresponding value.
                var solved;
```

```
            if (input === this.content) {
                    solved = true;
            } else {
                    solved = false;
            }
            this.solved = solved;
            return solved;
    }

    this.render = function () {
            push();
            if (this.solved === false) {
                    return;
            }
            fill(0, this.alpha);
            textAlign(CENTER, CENTER);
            translate(this.x, this.y);
            scale(this.scale);
            text(this.content, 0, 0);
            // increase the scale value by the increment
            value with each render
            this.scale = this.scale + this.scaleIncrement;
            // decrease the alpha value by the decrement
            value with each render
            this.alpha = this.alpha - this.alphaDecrement;
            pop();
    }
}
```

Our script is growing in size and complexity! Here in Listing 13-15 is the most recent function that we have added: getGameScore. It takes the score variable and loops through it to aggregate the number of wins and losses, as well as the total amount of guesses.

Listing 13-15. Calculating the game score using the getGameScore function

```
function getGameScore(score) {
        var wins = 0;
        var losses = 0;
        var total = score.length;

        for (var i = 0; i < total; i++) {
                var item = score[i];
                if (item === true) {
                        wins = wins+1;
                } else {
                        losses = losses+1;
                }
        }

        return {win: wins, loss: losses, total: total};
}
```

We added a conditional at the beginning of the draw function to check the results of the getGameScore function. If there are 3 losses or a total of 10 guesses, the conditional executes what basically has a return statement in it (Listing 13-16).

Listing 13-16. Conditionally stopping the game

```
var gameScore = getGameScore(results);
if (gameScore.loss === 3 || gameScore.total === 10) {
        return;
}
```

As seen in Listing 13-17, any line that comes after the return statement won't get executed since the current loop will terminate and a new one will begin - which will also terminate as long as the player's score remains the same.

Listing 13-17. Using the return statement to stop the draw loop

```
if (gameScore.loss === 3 || gameScore.total === 10) {
      return;
}
```

We need a mechanism to restart the game at this point. As shown in Listing 13-18, first, we will build a screen that is displayed when the game is over to display the player's score and prompt the player to press a key, ENTER, to restart the game (Figure 13-1). Secondly, we will make it so that if the player presses the ENTER key after the game is over, it will restart.

Listing 13-18. Restarting the game

```
var guessItem = null;
// controls the frequency that a new random number is
generated.
var interval = 100;
// an array to store solution values
var results = [];
var solution = null;
// stores if the game is over or not.
var gameOver = false;

function setup() {
      createCanvas(800, 300);
}

function draw() {
      var gameScore = getGameScore(results);
      if (gameScore.loss === 3 || gameScore.total === 10) {
            gameOver = true;
            displayGameOver(gameScore);
            return;
      }
```

```
        background(220);
        if (frameCount === 1 || frameCount % interval === 0) {
                solution = null;
                guessItem = new GuessItem(width/2, height/2, 1);
        }

        if (guessItem) {
                guessItem.render();
        }

        if (solution === true) {
                background(255);
        } else if (solution === false) {
                background(0);
        }
}

function displayGameOver(score) {
        // create the Game Over screen
        push();
        background(255);
        textSize(24);
        textAlign(CENTER, CENTER);
        translate(width / 2, height / 2);
        fill(237, 34, 93);
        text('GAME OVER!', 0, 0);
        translate(0, 36);
        fill(0);
        // have spaces inside the strings for the text to look
        proper.
        text('You have ' + score.win + ' correct guesses', 0, 0);
        translate(0, 100);
        textSize(16);
```

```
        var alternatingValue = map(sin(frameCount / 10), -1, 1,
        0, 255);
        fill(237, 34, 93, alternatingValue);
        text('PRESS ENTER', 0, 0);
        pop();
}

function getGameScore(score) {
        // given a score array, calculate the number of wins
        and losses.
        var wins = 0;
        var losses = 0;
        var total = score.length;

        for (var i = 0; i < total; i++) {
                var item = score[i];
                if (item === true) {
                        wins = wins+1;
                } else {
                        losses = losses+1;
                }
        }

        return {
                win: wins,
                loss: losses,
                total: total
        };
}

function restartTheGame() {
        // sets the game state to start.
        results = [];
```

```
        solution = null;
        gameOver = false;
}

function keyPressed() {
        // if game is over, then restart the game on ENTER key
        press.
        if (gameOver === true) {
                if (keyCode === ENTER) {
                        console.log('restart the game');
                        restartTheGame();
                        return;
                }
        }

        if (guessItem !== null) {
                // check to see if the pressed key matches to
                the displayed number.
                // if so set the solution global variable to a
                corresponding value.
                console.log('you pressed: ', key);
                solution = guessItem.solve(key);
                console.log(solution);
                if (solution) {
                        results.push(true);
                } else {
                        results.push(false);
                }
                guessItem = null;
        } else {
                console.log('nothing to be solved');
        }
}
```

```
function GuessItem(x, y, scl) {
        this.x = x;
        this.y = y;
        this.scale = scl;
        this.scaleIncrement = 0.5;
        this.content = getContent();
        this.alpha = 255;
        this.alphaDecrement = 3;
        this.solved = null;

        function getContent() {
                return String(parseInt(random(10), 10));
        }

        this.solve = function(input) {
                var solved;
                if (input === this.content) {
                        solved = true;
                } else {
                        solved = false;
                }
                this.solved = solved;
                return solved;
        }

        this.render = function() {
                push();
                if (this.solved === false) {
                        return;
                }
                fill(0, this.alpha);
                textAlign(CENTER, CENTER);
                translate(this.x, this.y);
```

```
            scale(this.scale);
            text(this.content, 0, 0);
            // increase the scale value by the increment
            value with each render
            this.scale = this.scale + this.scaleIncrement;
            // decrease the alpha value by the decrement
            value with each render
            this.alpha = this.alpha - this.alphaDecrement;
            pop();
        }
}
```

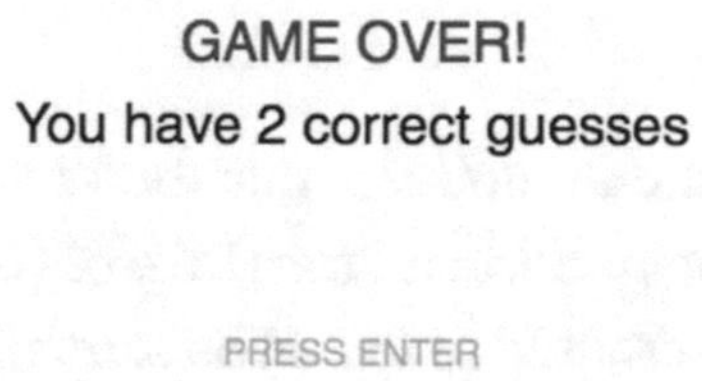

GAME OVER!
You have 2 correct guesses

PRESS ENTER

Figure 13-1. *Output from Listing 13-18*

Let's see what we did with the displayGameOver function first
(Listing 13-19). There are a couple of things happening here that we
didn't learn about before.

Listing 13-19. DisplayGameOver function

```
function displayGameOver(score) {
        push();
        background(255);
        textSize(24);
```

```
textAlign(CENTER, CENTER);
translate(width/2, height/2);
fill(237, 34, 93);
text('GAME OVER!', 0, 0);
translate(0, 36);
fill(0);
// have spaces inside the strings for the text to look
proper.
text('You have ' + score.win + ' correct guesses', 0, 0);
translate(0, 100);
textSize(16);
var alternatingValue = map(sin(frameCount/10), -1, 1,
0, 255);
fill(237, 34, 93, alternatingValue);
text('PRESS ENTER', 0, 0);
pop();
}
```

The first thing you should notice is that the translate function call results accumulate. If we perform a translate of (0, 100) after width/2, height/2, the resulting translate would be width/2, height/2 + 100.

Another thing that is new in this code is the p5.js sin and map functions that we are using to create a blinking text. A sin function calculates the sine of an angle. Given sequential values, the resulting sine value would alternate in between -1 and 1. But -1 and 1 are hardly useful to us as numeric values in our use case. A value that alternates in between 0 and 255 would be vastly more useful if we are to use this value to set the alpha of a fill function. This is where the map function comes into play (Listing 13-20). The map function maps the given value within the given range (second and third arguments) to the new given range (fourth and fifth arguments).

Listing 13-20. Using the map function

```
var alternatingValue = map(sin(frameCount/10), -1, 1, 0, 255);
```

We are mapping the result of the sin function that is in between -1 and 1 to 0 and 255.

Instead of simply executing a return statement, we can instead call this new function to display a message to the player. The next thing we implemented is a way to restart the game once it is over. For this, we require two things. First, we need a way to respond to the ENTER key. And then we need to re-initialize the relevant game variables to create the impression that a new game is starting.

Listing 13-21 shows the part of the keyPressed function that responds to the ENTER key.

Listing 13-21. Responding to the ENTER key

```
if (gameOver === true) {
        if (keyCode === ENTER) {
                console.log('restart the game');
                restartTheGame();
                return;
        }
}
```

We are using the keyCode variable alongside with the ENTER variable to respond to the ENTER key press.

The contents of the restartTheGame function are simple (Listing 13-22). It just re-initializes a couple of variables that are in global scope such as the user score to make it start working again.

Listing 13-22. The restartTheGame function

```
function restartTheGame() {
        // sets the game state to start.
        results = [];
```

```
        solution = null;
        gameOver = false;
}
```

And this is it! We could keep working on it to make the game experience much better by tweaking the mechanics and enhancing the visuals of the game. But we have laid down the foundation that makes up the skeleton of our game, which can now be developed further according to your specific needs.

Final Code

This is the final code (Listing 13-23). I decided to do a couple of updates for the version I was working on. Instead of displaying numbers, I decided to display the words for the numbers. I find that to be more visually pleasing and also more challenging from a gameplay point of view, as it adds a bit of an overhead to parsing what you see. I also added a new method into the GuessItem called drawEllipse that draws ellipses on the screen along with the words for a more visually engaging game. Finally, I tweaked the game parameters a bit to make the timing right and added messages to be displayed whenever the player enters a right or wrong number Figure 13-2 shows a screen from the final game code.

Listing 13-23. The final code

```
var guessItem = null;
// controls the frequency that a new random number is
generated.
var interval = 60; // changing this to make the game feel
                   faster.
// an array to store solution values
var results = [];
var solution = null;
```

```
// stores if the game is over or not.
var gameOver = false;

function setup() {
        createCanvas(800, 300);
}

function draw() {
        // if there are 3 losses or 10 attempts stop the game.
        var gameScore = getGameScore(results);
        if (gameScore.loss === 3 || gameScore.total === 10) {
                gameOver = true;
                displayGameOver(gameScore);
                return;
        }
        background(0); // black background
        if (frameCount === 1 || frameCount % interval === 0) {
                solution = null;
                guessItem = new GuessItem(width/2, height/2, 1);
        }

        if (guessItem) {
                guessItem.render();
        }

        if (solution == true || solution === false) {
                // displaying a text on screen instead of flat
                color.
                solutionMessage(gameScore.total, solution);
        }

}
```

```javascript
function solutionMessage(seed, solution) {
        // display a random message based on a true of false
        solution.
        var trueMessages = [
                'GOOD JOB!',
                'DOING GREAT!',
                'OMG!',
                'SUCH WIN!',
                'I APPRECIATE YOU',
                'IMPRESSIVE'
        ];

        var falseMessages = [
                'OH NO!',
                'BETTER LUCK NEXT TIME!',
                'PFTTTT',
                ':('
        ];

        var messages;

        push();
        textAlign(CENTER, CENTER);
        fill(237, 34, 93);
        textSize(36);
        randomSeed(seed * 10000);

        if (solution === true) {
                background(255);
                messages = trueMessages;
        } else if (solution === false) {
                background(0);
                messages = falseMessages;
        }
```

```
    text(messages[parseInt(random(messages.length), 10)],
    width / 2, height / 2);
    pop();
}

function displayGameOver(score) {
    // create the Game Over screen
    push();
    background(255);
    textSize(24);
    textAlign(CENTER, CENTER);
    translate(width / 2, height / 2);
    fill(237, 34, 93);
    text('GAME OVER!', 0, 0);
    translate(0, 36);
    fill(0);
    // have spaces inside the string for the text to look
    proper.
    text('You have ' + score.win + ' correct guesses', 0, 0);
    translate(0, 100);
    textSize(16);
    var alternatingValue = map(sin(frameCount / 10), -1, 1,
    0, 255);
    fill(237, 34, 93, alternatingValue);
    text('PRESS ENTER', 0, 0);
    pop();
}

function getGameScore(score) {
    // given a score array, calculate the number of wins
    and losses.
    var wins = 0;
    var losses = 0;
    var total = score.length;
```

```
        for (var i = 0; i < total; i++) {
                var item = score[i];
                if (item === true) {
                        wins = wins + 1;
                } else {
                        losses = losses + 1;
                }
        }

        return {
                win: wins,
                loss: losses,
                total: total
        };
}

function restartTheGame() {
        // sets the game state to start.
        results = [];
        solution = null;
        gameOver = false;
}

function keyPressed() {
        // if game is over, then restart the game on ENTER key
        press.
        if (gameOver === true) {
                if (keyCode === ENTER) {
                        console.log('restart the game');
                        restartTheGame();
                        return;
                }
        }
```

```
        if (guessItem !== null) {
                // check to see if the pressed key matches to
                the displayed number.
                // if so set the solution global variable to a
                corresponding value.
                console.log('you pressed: ', key);
                solution = guessItem.solve(key);
                console.log(solution);
                if (solution) {
                        results.push(true);
                } else {
                        results.push(false);
                }
                guessItem = null;
        } else {
                console.log('nothing to be solved');
        }
}

function GuessItem(x, y, scl) {
        this.x = x;
        this.y = y;
        this.scale = scl;
        this.scaleIncrement = 0.25;
        this.clr = 255;
        this.content = getContent();
        this.alpha = 255;
        this.alphaDecrement = 6;
        this.solved = null;
        this.contentMap = {
                '1': 'one',
                '2': 'two',
```

```
                '3': 'three',
                '4': 'four',
                '5': 'five',
                '6': 'six',
                '7': 'seven',
                '8': 'eight',
                '9': 'nine',
                '0': 'zero'
        };
        this.colors = [
                [63, 184, 175],
                [127, 199, 175],
                [218, 216, 167],
                [255, 158, 157],
                [255, 61, 127],
                [55, 191, 211],
                [159, 223, 82],
                [234, 209, 43],
                [250, 69, 8],
                [194, 13, 0]
        ];

        function getContent() {
                // generate a random integer in between 0 and 9
                return String(parseInt(random(10), 10));
        }

        this.solve = function(input) {
                // check to see if the given input is
                equivalent to the content.
                // set solved to the corresponding value.
                var solved;
```

```
        if (input === this.content) {
                solved = true;
        } else {
                solved = false;
        }
        this.solved = solved;
        return solved;
}

this.drawEllipse = function(size, strkWeight,
speedMultiplier, seed) {
        // draw an animated ellipse with a random color
        to the screen.
        push();
        randomSeed(seed);
        translate(this.x, this.y);
        var ellipseSize = this.scale * speedMultiplier;
        scale(ellipseSize);
        var clr = this.colors[parseInt(random(this.
        colors.length), 10)]
        stroke(clr);
        noFill();
        strokeWeight(strkWeight);
        ellipse(0, 0, size, size);
        pop();
}

this.render = function() {
        push();
        this.drawEllipse(100, 15, 2, 1 * this.content *
        1000);
        this.drawEllipse(60, 7, 2, 1 * this.content *
        2000);
```

```
this.drawEllipse(35, 3, 1.2, 1 * this.content *
3000);
pop();

push();
fill(this.clr, this.alpha);
textAlign(CENTER, CENTER);
translate(this.x, this.y);
scale(this.scale);
 // display the word for the corresponding number
text(this.contentMap[this.content], 0, 0);
// increase the scale value by the increment
value with each render
this.scale = this.scale + this.scaleIncrement;
// decrease the alpha value by the decrement
value with each render
this.alpha = this.alpha - this.alphaDecrement;
pop();
    }
}
```

Figure 13-2. *Screen from the final game code*

The biggest change to the code is the solutionMessage function so let's take a look at that in a bit more detail (Listing 13-24). Previously we were just using an if-else statement based on the value of the solution variable to decide what to display on screen. If the solution was true, we were displaying a white background, and if the solution was false, we were displaying a black background.

Now if the solution is either of these values (true or false), we are passing it to a function called solutionMessage, which chooses a random message to display using gameScore.total as a seed for the random function.

Listing 13-24. Displaying a message on the screen

```
if (solution == true || solution === false) {
        solutionMessage(gameScore.total, solution);
}
```

As seen in Listing 13-25, inside the solutionMessage function, there are two arrays with a bunch of message values that are to be displayed based on the value of the solution.

Listing 13-25. Conditionally choosing a message

```
if (solution === true) {
        background(255);
        messages = trueMessages;
} else if (solution === false) {
        background(0);
        messages = falseMessages;
}
```

In Listing 13-26, we pick a random value from these arrays by converting the return value of the random function to an integer.

Listing 13-26. Choosing a random message

```
text(messages[parseInt(random(messages.length), 10)], width / 2,
height / 2);
```

Summary

This was definitely a challenging example that put everything we learned so far to the test.

It is very impressive that we can build a game by just using p5.js that can run on the web and can be played by millions of people. And it wasn't all that difficult as well; the entire program is just around 200 lines. There is certainly room for improvement where we can make the game difficulty dynamic based on the player's performance, add more visual flair and add a dynamic scoring system where we can assign different points to correct guesses based on the amount of time it took to guess a number. The game can be converted to display words instead of numbers. It can show images that you need to type the name for or calculations that you need to answer. The possibilities are numerous!

Having said that, p5.js might not be the best platform to create games with if we wanted to build more advanced projects. A proper game library would come with features such as an asset loading system, sprite support, collision detection, physics engine, particle systems… which is more often than not required when building advanced games. This is not to say you can't use p5.js to build a game, though. We just proved that it is entirely possible. It is just that there are other libraries out there that are more specialized around that solution whereas p5.js is more tailored towards creating interactive, animated experiences on the web. But by learning p5.js, you are not only learning how to use JavaScript and all the things that it is great at, but you are also developing an understanding for working with other 3rd party libraries in the JavaScript ecosystem.

APPENDIX

Final Words

Having completed this book, you should now be familiar with the basics of the JavaScript language and with programming in general since the concepts we learned are widely applicable to different programming languages.

Think of learning what past tense is, in a natural, spoken, language like in English. How you construct a past tense sentence might structurally differ between English and Japanese, but the fact that you have a conceptual understanding of what past tense is would allow you to transfer your knowledge from one language to the next in a much easier manner once you figure out the mapping in between them.

In this book, we learned about the fundamental structures in programming languages such as variables, operators, loops, conditionals, functions, objects, and arrays using JavaScript. All the programming languages that I personally had to interface so far had an implementation of these concepts in one way or another. The syntax for them might differ but the workings are pretty similar. Generally speaking, the knowledge you acquire in one programming language is highly transferrable to other languages.

Alongside JavaScript, we also learned about the p5.js library along the way. This means that if you wanted to utilize your newly found programming knowledge, you could continue to do so by using p5.js with great comfort.

The thing that is currently missing from our knowledge is how to deploy our work on the Web, thereby sharing it with the rest of the world. Since this has been a book focused on learning how to program, I didn't

© Engin Arslan 2018
E. Arslan, *Learn JavaScript with p5.js*, https://doi.org/10.1007/978-1-4842-3426-6

want to burden us with secondary, operational, concerns like these. There are already great resources out there on building applications on the Web.

You might find yourself constrained a bit at this point, especially if you don't want to keep sharpening your newly acquired skills in p5.js. Where should one go next from here?

Where to Go Next

As I mentioned at the beginning of the book, learning JavaScript will open a world of opportunities in front of you as there are a lot of domains where you can apply your knowledge. Where to go next surely depends on where you would like to grow your skill set in.

If you want to move beyond p5.js and create user-facing web applications, you will surely need to learn the basics of HTML and CSS to build graphical interfaces for your projects. The Additional Resources section at the end of the Appendix is a good place to start.

After that, learning some DOM API would be useful to be able to hook up the interface elements on the page to execute JavaScript commands. If you wanted to build slightly more complicated interfaces, then jQuery might help as it makes working with JavaScript slightly easier when working with web pages. If you are looking to build more advanced interfaces where there are lots of interactions and state dependencies in between page elements, then a front-end framework such as Angular or a library like React can be very useful. I would suggest not rushing to learn these tools even though they are all the hype nowadays. Starting out with pure JavaScript and then moving to jQuery to build slightly more challenging interfaces will help you appreciate the problems that these more complicated tools are built to solve.

Maybe you might want to do some server-side programming. Then Node.js is the tool that you should pick up. Server-side programming might involve any back-end calculations that don't need to happen on the client side, on the browser, and might involve building scripts that interface with the operating system of the host computer to do things like creating files and folders, deleting them, etc. A `Node.js` script doesn't necessarily need to be in service of a web application back end. The prime advantage of Node.js is that it provides you with an environment on your machine, rather than on the browser, to run JavaScript in. Node.js sets the JavaScript free from the constraints of the browser environment. For example, there is `Electron`. It is a `Node.js`-based framework that allows you to build native desktop applications using web technologies. You can use `Electron` to build a web browser using JavaScript rather than to build something on the browser using JavaScript!

Automating web pages, programmatically connecting to the Internet, and scraping online data might be your thing. For that, there is `Casper.js` and `Puppeteer`. If you wanted to do advanced data visualizations, then you should check out the D3 library. Maybe you want to get into robotics, or program IOT devices using JavaScript. How about giving `Johnny-Five` a try then? You can build native mobile apps (`React Native`), HTML5 games (`Phaser`), databases (`mongoDB`) 3D visuals, and animations (`Three.js`), or even cognitive applications that make use of Artificial Intelligence (`IBM Watson`) all by using JavaScript. See the Additional Resources section for links to all these resources.

When learning a new programming language it is best to have a plan: a vision for something that you would like to build. Ideally, build the minimum viable project that you can lift off the ground without encumbering yourself with too much work or too many technicalities. It's about getting to that point and then building the next thing – always getting better, always learning something new. Welcome to the world of programming. I can't wait to see what you will come up with.

Additional Resources

- HTML - `https://developer.mozilla.org/en-US/docs/Web/HTML`

- CSS - `https://developer.mozilla.org/en-US/docs/Web/CSS`

- DOM API - `https://developer.mozilla.org/en-US/docs/Web/API/Document_Object_Model`

- jQuery - `https://jquery.com/`

- Angular - `https://angular.io/`

- React - `https://reactjs.org/`

- Node.js - `https://nodejs.org/en/`

- Electron - `https://electronjs.org/`

- CasperJS - `http://casperjs.org/`

- Puppeteer - `https://github.com/GoogleChrome/puppeteer`

- D3.js - `https://d3js.org/`

- Johnny-Five - `http://johnny-five.io/`

- React Native - `https://facebook.github.io/react-native/`

- Phaser - `https://phaser.io/`

- MongoDB - `https://mongodb.github.io/node-mongodb-native/`

- Three.js - `https://threejs.org/`

- IBM Watson - `https://www.ibm.com/watson/products-services/`

Index

A, B

Arrays

C

D

E

© Engin Arslan 2018
E. Arslan, *Learn JavaScript with p5.js*, https://doi.org/10.1007/978-1-4842-3426-6

Get the eBook for only $5!

Why limit yourself?

With most of our titles available in both PDF and ePUB format, you can access your content wherever and however you wish—on your PC, phone, tablet, or reader.

Since you've purchased this print book, we are happy to offer you the eBook for just $5.

To learn more, go to http://www.apress.com/companion or contact support@apress.com.

Apress®

Printed in the United States
By Bookmasters